"*Forgiveness after Trauma* pro[vides] and clarity on one of the most significant issues su[rvivors] as they take steps toward safety and recovery. Confusion, harmful messages, and stigmas surrounding the topic of forgiveness have often been obstacles and pitfalls on the path to freedom. Susannah Griffith helps us understand what it really means to forgive after trauma. She destigmatizes anger, extends permission and invitation to lament, answers many important questions about accountability and reconciliation, and gives hope for the future. She has taken a depth of personal experience, loving care, and profound expertise to write a book that will empower many who find themselves stuck and unsure how to move forward on their healing journey."

—**Wade Mullen,** author of *Something's Not Right: Decoding the Hidden Tactics of Abuse—and Freeing Yourself from Its Power*

"In *Forgiveness after Trauma*, Griffith weaves together Scripture, memoir, and practical theology in a trauma-informed ethic of forgiveness. Her compelling, nuanced writing is required reading for clergy, lay leaders, and anyone willing to accompany survivors navigating intimate partner violence."

—**Teresa Kim Pecinovsky,** author of *Mother God*

"Through her own story of trauma and recovery, Susannah Griffith gently urges readers to discover the many facets of forgiveness, paving a way forward after harm. On her journey she leaves no stone unturned: addressing anger, lament, accountability, and empathy. Her story is one I'll return to again and again."

—**Tiffany Bluhm,** speaker and author of *Prey Tell: Why We Silence Women Who Tell the Truth and How Everyone Can Speak Up*

"In *Forgiveness after Trauma*, Susannah Griffith speaks from a mixture of personal narrative, biblical scholarship, and pastoral experience to deliver a trauma-informed understanding of forgiveness. Griffith offers the church an opportunity to re-shape its approach to reconciliation and forgiveness in order to better support those who have experienced trauma. While books on forgiveness abound, I have not come across one like *Forgiveness after Trauma*."

—**J.W. Buck**, author of *Everyday Activism: Following 7 Practices of Jesus to Create a Just World*

forgiveness
after
trauma

Also by the Author

*Leaving Silence: Sexualized Violence, the Bible,
and Standing with Survivors*

forgiveness
after
trauma

A Path to Find
Healing and Empowerment

SUSANNAH GRIFFITH

BrazosPress
a division of Baker Publishing Group
Grand Rapids, Michigan

Published by Brazos Press
a division of Baker Publishing Group
Grand Rapids, Michigan
BrazosPress.com

Printed in the United States of America

Library of Congress Cataloging-in-Publication Data
Names: Griffith, Susannah, 1990– author.
Title: Forgiveness after trauma : a path to find healing and empowerment / Susannah Griffith.
Description: Grand Rapids, Michigan : Brazos Press, a division of Baker Publishing Group, [2024] | Includes bibliographical references.
Identifiers: LCCN 2023030484 | ISBN 9781587435973 (paperback) | ISBN 9781587436277 (casebound) | ISBN 9781493444960 (ebook)
Subjects: LCSH: Forgiveness—Religious aspects—Christianity. | Forgiveness—Religious aspects—Christianity—Biblical teaching.
Classification: LCC BV4647.F55 G76 2024 | DDC 234/.5—dc23/eng/20230831
LC record available at https://lccn.loc.gov/2023030484

24 25 26 27 28 29 30   7 6 5 4 3 2 1

For all people
who live in the bondage of abuse,
who have been told to forgive and stay.

May you know that life is your birthright,
in the name of God.

contents

introduction

Frankly, I wish forgiveness was a concept I thought less about. But it has dogged me much of my life. On a moonlit walk around the lake on my college campus, my boyfriend at the time asked me what my biggest theological question was. I remember telling him it was about forgiveness: I couldn't quite figure out what it was or how to do it. I couldn't align my awareness that certain abuses would never be okay with my belief that Scripture asks us to forgive offenders. And that was even before what I came to understand as the worst happened.

In May 2015, I married my seminary sweetheart, a man who was and is affectionate, creative, sensitive, intelligent, and a little quirky. Neill had wooed me with his love for the Myers-Briggs Personality Inventory and his knack for beautifully expressing atonement theology. We were ideal companions for each other, matching wit for wit, innocence for innocence, and passion for passion. From the outside, everything was perfect; we were, as my older brother once said to me, "peas and carrots." Our companionship and the beautiful children we eventually shared were all I'd ever wanted.

But a painful side of our relationship grew that few people knew about. The trauma that ensued from our relationship was all the more shocking and disturbing to me because of the depth of trust and innocence I'd previously experienced with Neill. He, I'd always believed, was different from those who had harmed me in the past. I never thought he would hurt me. But Neill's mental health issues, long existing but dormant, began manifesting in more and more concerning ways. A year into our marriage, he pulled a knife out of the dishwasher and pressed it to his throat during an argument, holding, it seemed, my own life for ransom along with his own. As scared and shaken as I was, this was only a brief foreshadowing of what was to come. A little over a year after that, he was physically violent toward me for the first time. At that moment, a resounding truth emerged from me: "Our marriage is over." I knew as soon as the physical harm happened that it was, for me, a line in the sand that once crossed represented a point of no return. This truth seemed straightforward, but figuring out what to do with that truth moving forward was anything but. "I'm gonna kill you," he hissed back at me before jumping off the balcony of our apartment.

More suicide attempts, more physical abuse, and more escalation followed, each instance inching us a little closer to his death and my own. My expressed desire to leave the relationship in response to the abuse, sometimes spoken in anger, was what most often precipitated his episodes of instability. This fact was a source of confusion for me, because as trapped as I felt, I believed that if I said nothing, his behavior would stay in a safe realm. Yet time after time, I found myself trying to restabilize him after these episodes, their terrifying tenor making me feel that both of our lives were on the line.

During the most intense year of this pattern, my health fell apart. For a span of many months, I lost the ability to sleep at night. I developed autoimmune diseases. Perhaps most dramatically, my water broke during one of Neill's episodes, and I experienced unmedicated labor and birth, weeks early, of our second child—the pain of labor compounded by the trauma that had just preceded it. When Child Protective Services arrived at our apartment in response to a report of domestic violence, the caseworker threatened to remove our children from *me* as a result of *my* traumatizing them, asking me, "What did you do that caused your husband to hurt you?" and warning me that if they got wind of future events in our home, *I* would lose our children, despite my repeated attempts to separate safely from Neill. Because the caseworker heard a different story from Neill, my words fell on closed ears. Though I have always kept our children in my custody, I have not been freed from the intense fear of losing them one day as a result of his behavior. The consequences of Neill's actions were, for me, catastrophic, and I have continued to discover new effects.

I believe I did what I could at that time to protect myself and my babies. Most fundamentally, I kept our lives running no matter what was happening with Neill, making sure there was a roof over our heads, the bills were paid, and food was on the table. I persevered in my doctoral program, knowing that if I had a PhD and could get an academic job, I'd have a ticket to greater autonomy. I sought multiple avenues of support, but few people significantly helped me during the first few years of my struggle. Again and again, I encountered blame from many people around me. I was asked to simply avoid doing anything that could trigger his anger. I was asked why I was pregnant with another of his children if the problem was really so bad. I was instructed not to hurt him by saying I wanted to leave. I was told that my selfishness or my need to assert my will was the root problem. I was told that if only we could reconcile—and this was often the prayed-for outcome—we would be a great testimony to the power of marriage. What I wanted and needed were never the focus. Instead, everyone's concern revolved around whatever would stabilize Neill the most.

As a graduate student, especially one with small children, for the first several years of this story I felt stymied by my lack of financial resources. Nevertheless, Neill and I separated multiple times as I sought safety for myself and our daughters. Each time, Neill returned with heartfelt promises of change. I insisted he pursue professional help, which he did. Yet his troubling behavior still cropped up from time to time, and I had the unyielding sense that something was still deeply broken, both in our relationship and in our own reflections on what had transpired.

I bided my time for a moment when I would have the financial and career stability to act more decisively, and after I had been working for a few months as a tenure-track professor, my moment arrived. Neill's last suicide attempt summoned in me a new, steely resolve never to tolerate the emotional roller coaster of his behavior again. I separated from Neill and filed for divorce, not intending to reunite. I purchased a house solely in my name, one of the most empowering acts of my life. I gave birth to our third child without him by my side out of respect for my body's boundaries. But after that longer period of complete separation (about six months), Neill's work to change seemed to stick. He became one of the very few people I have heard of who acted abusively and took responsibility for changing their behavior, which set him apart from others in my past who harmed me. He began to know who he was outside of our relationship and to show greater emotional stability.

We decided to continue our relationship in this new state of change. We renewed our vows in the presence of our dear friends, Lucas and Penelope, who feature prominently in this forgiveness story. The passion, the companionship, and the meeting of the minds and hearts were still there. We still enjoyed deep theological and political conversations, delicious meals prepared together, and a good binge of our favorite TV shows. We gladly and generously supported each other's emerging careers and joyfully watched our children grow. Best friends and co-parents we could easily be, in spite of what had passed between us. But, for me, the pain of being married to a man who had tried to take my life returned quickly after our reunion. The knowledge that he had so utterly betrayed me, again and again, wedged its way between us no matter the affection I felt for him.

Ultimately, I came to a point of knowing I could not continue on as we had been. I was living two lives. At home, as long as I never brought up the pain of the past, we enjoyed a pleasant and pragmatic companionship, sharing a roof and our children. But identifying myself as part of a married unit outside our home was something I struggled to do. I could not wear my wedding ring without perceiving it as a noose. I could not bear to take our sweet baby girl to the church together to dedicate her. The truth was that inside myself I knew, vow renewal or no vow renewal, the marriage still felt haunted.

What was wrong with me? He had done everything I had asked him to do. He had made the changes that were needed, it seemed. I felt confident that he was no longer a threat to me. Part of me wanted a life with him—to overcome the resistance, to keep giving the marriage a chance, to find out definitively if a life with him was possible in spite of all the history. But an even bigger part of me felt a gut-level resistance to an intimate relationship with him.

By the end of 2021, facing down another year into my thirties, I knew I had to decide whether to stay or leave, for the sake of not just Neill and me but also our three daughters, the oldest of whom was rapidly growing aware of the dynamics of our family life. I felt that I'd tried all the conventional methods for relational healing and discernment and that I needed a sign straight from God telling me what to do next. I especially felt I needed some divine intervention if I was going to do something other than finalize the divorce I had started during our last separation.

Lucas and Penelope were family friends and also a ministry couple known for their open doors to stragglers like me, an above-average tea selection, and equal degrees of warmth and wisdom. Though many others who had come alongside Neill and me on this journey had been scared away—by the severity and intensity of the mental health and violence concerns, by my indecision, and by the spiritual meta-questions the situation evoked—Lucas and Penelope had stayed close by and, miraculously, remained friends with both Neill and me. Through the long period of separation and beyond, Lucas and Penelope had sat with me, listened to me, wept with me, fed me, prayed for me, and even supported me during my labor with our third daughter. They had earned my trust enough to say things to me that I wouldn't have tolerated from other people. For months, they listened to my anguish and confusion about the direction I wanted the relationship to go. Then, with trepidation, Lucas brought up the *F* word.

"Susannah, we've talked a lot about many things, but I don't think we've ever talked about . . . and I want to be really cautious bringing this up, because I know this word can be used in a spiritually abusive way, and I want to make sure we never do that to you . . . but what are your thoughts about forgiveness? What if we—you, me, and Penelope—went on a journey of learning what forgiveness is together?"

Maybe that was it. Maybe forgiveness could resolve the pain I felt in my relationship with Neill. Maybe if I could forgive him, then our relationship and our family could be whole again.

Trusting my friends deeply, I agreed to embark on a journey of learning what forgiveness is and is not, exploring what it means to forgive as a Christian believer. As a lifelong Christian and a biblical scholar, I realized at the outset that I didn't know much about forgiveness, and that lacuna of knowledge felt a little shocking. *Forgiveness* is a word that gets thrown around a lot, but discussing what it actually entails—landing on a livable definition—always felt out of reach to me. Frankly, I tried to avoid the topic as long as I could.

When I thought about forgiveness in the Bible, the following verses came to mind first:

> For if you forgive others their trespasses, your heavenly Father will also forgive you, but if you do not forgive others, neither will your Father forgive your trespasses. (Matt. 6:14–15)

> Then Peter came and said to him, "Lord, if my brother or sister sins against me, how often should I forgive? As many as seven times?" Jesus said to him, "Not seven times, but, I tell you, seventy-seven times." (Matt. 18:21–22)

Those words were painful for me to read at the outset. Christians have certainly weaponized them in ways that have been harmful to trauma survivors. Throughout my experiences of trauma, I'd often felt Christ close to me, suffering with me, advocating for me. But reading those verses, I felt that I was encountering a Jesus I barely knew, a Jesus who didn't take seriously how deeply I'd been harmed or a Jesus who wanted me to let my abuser off the hook. That Jesus wasn't someone I could honestly follow. But that's not who I thought Jesus was.

I realized I needed to look more deeply into forgiveness, and it was easier to define it based on what it is *not* than what it *is*. I knew that my lived experiences and the lived experiences of other survivors had to matter. I knew that Jesus, who died as an abuse victim, had to understand what I and so many others had suffered. Surely the one who loves me beyond the love of all others would not prescribe something harmful to me, such as the harm I'd experienced through the words about forgiveness I'd heard along the way. I had to reject those abusive teachings on forgiveness from the start:

- Forgiveness did not mean I had to stay in or return to a relationship that was harmful.
- Forgiveness did not mean erasing the past or its memory.
- Forgiveness did not mean all the wounds of the past were automatically healed.
- Forgiveness did not mean that anger had no place or that consequences were inappropriate.
- Forgiveness did not mean I ceded my right to talk about the past and process my experiences.
- Forgiveness did not mean I had been guilty of harming myself by carrying the memories of what had happened and not letting them go.
- Forgiveness did not mean, necessarily, reconciliation.

Naming these demons of false forgiveness, acknowledging the harm they'd caused, and dispelling them was the only way for me to reach a place where I could begin to understand what forgiveness could mean for me in my situation.

Together, then, my friends and I began exploring forgiveness in ways that felt safe, authentic, and life-giving. We began to seek a deeper understanding of forgiveness, plumbing the Bible for the justice, remembrance, and healing elements of forgiveness that I, as a survivor, needed to find for it to be relevant to me. What I discovered is that when we expand beyond the usual suspects in consulting biblical resources, we can create the nuanced, compassionate portrait of forgiveness that so many of us are searching for. I settled on a few principles, recognizing that forgiveness holds safely the realities of trauma that I carried in my body, mind, and spirit. Here are those guiding principles:

- *Forgiveness requires physical and emotional safety.* It is not a process we can undertake when traumatic experiences press too closely on us. The cues of trauma must be attended to, letting us know at any time when harm is too immediate to explore forgiveness.

- *Forgiveness needs to be based in the reality of what happened.* Forgiveness that perpetuates the lies of abuse and its justification is not forgiveness at all.

- *Forgiveness needs to come from a place of communal empathy.* Too often, those who survive violence bear the additional burden of being expected to carry the weight of forgiveness alone. No one should carry it alone.

- *Forgiveness allows for lament.* The profound unfairness of what has happened requires attention and witness, from ourselves and from others.

- *Forgiveness must be centered on the experience of the person who received the harm.* Forgiveness is meaningful to survivors if it leads to life and defies the death-dealing experiences of abuse they have suffered.

I believe that Lucas and Penelope initially launched this forgiveness journey out of a hope of restoring my relationship with Neill. Some of the ideas about forgiveness that I have now rejected may have motivated their initial work with me; however, together we found ways through these misunderstandings of forgiveness. Through my biblical study and life experience, forgiveness has come to mean placing responsibility for healing the past at the throne of God, who is justice and mercy. There is a time and a place for every emotion, every move toward safety, every insistence on accountability, and every relationship boundary that I, as a survivor of intimate partner violence, have experienced on my journey toward recovery. And yet even after I have taken all those vital steps, there may not necessarily be a sense of peace or wholeness. Nothing in this world can restore, fully, the wrong that happened, the harm it caused, and what was taken away from me during those terrible days and nights. Those losses and that injustice will still be there no matter what Neill does or what I do for the rest of our lives.

But day by day, in my reality of safety and trauma recovery, I picture God in Christ carrying on my behalf those injustices and wounds that I cannot bear, doing with them whatever must be done. I do not pretend that all is made right or that the terrible events never happened. But I know that the rightly kept record of wrongs is safe in the arms of the one who is more passionate about my justice and healing than I am. My laments about the pain that both Neill and I experienced, the relational destruction it produced, and its aftermath are surpassed only by the laments of the Holy Spirit, who intercedes for us with "groanings too deep for words" (Rom. 8:26). If God holds all that for me, then perhaps little by little I can step away from the immediacy of the past and rest assured that divine attention will address what remains unresolved and needed. That is the forgiveness I am choosing. The journey isn't done, and, relationally, it might not end the way you think it should.

I don't have all the answers, but exploring forgiveness has been deeply meaningful and transformative in the ways that I relate to the pain of my past. In this book, I want to share parts of my journey paired with reflections based on my background as a biblical scholar to make available forgiveness paths different from the harmful ones so often proffered in the name of God. In the first chapter, I explore the most commonly cited biblical verses about forgiveness in light of their troubling and potentially less-troubling interpretations, then in each subsequent chapter, I expand on crucial forgiveness-related themes from biblical texts that have shaped my own forgiveness journey as a trauma survivor.

The work on forgiveness I'm exploring here follows up as a sequitur not only to my personal experiences but also to my previous book, *Leaving Silence: Sexualized Violence, the Bible, and Standing with Survivors*. *Leaving Silence* explores how the Bible portrays sexualized violence and how survivors of sexualized violence and those who care for them can reclaim Scripture as a source of healing and hope in spite of the painful ways these stories have figured into Christian interpretation. But in *Leaving Silence*, I intentionally stayed away from the subject of forgiveness. There was too much content concerning abuses of power in the Bible to get into how we might respond with forgiveness or non-forgiveness once events are farther in the rearview mirror. I also didn't want to shift the focus from survivors and their needs to the demands that church and societal communities often place on survivors to forgive. But now I see that I must attend to these problems too.

When I study the Bible, I seek to bring together approaches that pay attention to the historical and cultural contexts "behind the text," the literary features "within the text," and the realities of here and now that contemporary survivors of abuse navigate "in front of the text." When I engage with the Bible as a biblical scholar, I want to do justice to the biblical texts, reading them with the respect they deserve as the faith testimony of those who are my forebears and yet who come from a time and place very different from my own. Recognizing how Christians have often overlooked the Old Testament, I especially want to examine the whole (Protestant) canon as my source of inspiration. I also want to do justice for survivors of power-based violence, many of whom, like me, have experienced deep harm through legacies of biblical interpretation. At my best as an interpreter of the Bible, I believe that reading the Bible justly means holding in balance all these valid concerns.

As a biblical scholar, I realize I don't (and *can't*) check my own lived experiences at the door. Rather, through naming my own investments, I seek to provide clarity for readers about the work I'm doing. If I were to give a name to the kind of scholarship I'm producing, I would call it *theological, trauma-informed, feminist biblical interpretation*. That means, to me, a few things. First, I read as a Christian who regards the Bible as divinely inspired, and the work of biblical interpretation that I do contributes to the way I conceptualize God's relationship with the world. Second, I seek to center the experiences and voices of trauma survivors in my work. I regard trauma not as a stigmatizing diagnosis but as an adaptive reality of how our bodies, emotions, and spirits seek to survive in a world shattered by circumstances outside of our control. Third, I read the Bible with an awareness of power dynamics created through unequal systems of human relationships, such as patriarchy, which negatively affect people of all gender identities. My identity as a woman and my experiences living in my female body are crucial to this aspect of my work, and I know my frame of reference is limited.

Forgiveness is a huge topic, and I can't cover every scenario that produces a desire or need to forgive. Forgiveness may enter the discussion any time harm is involved—and harm can take place in basically any human relationship! While recognizing that so much territory could be covered, I focus specifically on situations of abuse. Abuse is especially thorny when it comes to forgiveness because, like other offenses, it contains harm. *But what's crucial in an abusive dynamic is that harm is inflicted through power differences.* In my story with my husband, the difference in power between us that led to harm had to do with gender and accompanying physical strength. (My story is about male-to-female abuse, but female-to-male abuse and abuse in same-sex relationships happen too.) Abuse involves using power unfairly to gain control over others, and it appears in myriad forms. Knowing how frequently Christians hurl the Bible at abuse survivors in the name of "forgiveness," I feel a responsibility to address this topic.

This isn't a how-to book. I have no idea how to forgive someone, but I know that in my life forgiveness has happened.

I hope that in my story others can find points of resonance, hope, and encouragement. I offer my story not as advice (I don't know what you should do!) but because I believe the story I can tell *now* could have saved me a lot of pain *then*.

My story is intimately linked to God's story in Scripture. As a Christian minister, scholar, writer, and trauma survivor, I want to bring others alongside me on this journey of reclaiming the whole Bible as *a* liberating Word. The Bible represents one aspect of *the* Word who is Jesus Christ, the cornerstone of our faith who, taking on blessed and bruised human flesh, demonstrates God's solidarity with the trauma of the world (John 1:14; 1 Cor. 3:11). I think that God's solidarity with the world changes everything, including my own trauma. In all I write, I hope I point to the love of God, whose will never includes abuse and who desires justice for the vulnerable. Reconciliation is the work of this God and not the burden of any survivor. I pray that in your journey you know the love of the God who carries what each of us can no longer bear to hold.

biblical forgiveness(es)

not what I thought

An Unforgiving Christian?

The summer I turned nineteen, I felt a need to reckon with someone who had both harmed me deeply and done much good in my life. I decided to set new boundaries with this person. Predictably, when I set these new boundaries and confronted this person with what they had done, the whole family system that relied on shame, silence, and protecting those responsible went into disarray. I got a long email from a loved one about the fault I bore in causing this disruption to our family equilibrium. Truthfully, I deleted the email a long time ago (this was before it occurred to me that I might write a book on the topic of forgiveness), but I will never forget the gist of one of the lines: "You claim to be a Christian, but if you want to live up to this name, you have to stop what you're doing and forgive."

The writer of the email was not a Christian (ironically) but wanted to tell me how to be one for the sake of maintaining an abusive relationship. She had herself experienced abuse in the family dynamic she was defending. The email conveyed that Christian forgiveness means abnegating the right to talk about and resist experiences of abuse. Because my confrontation with abusive authority and my reluctance to stay in an abusive relationship caused pain, my action had to be inappropriate and un-Christian.

A few months later, I found myself unprotected in a situation where I was in close proximity to the person who had harmed me, whose influence I had long tried to escape. This person asked me on the spot, "I know you've had trouble in the past feeling like we could move forward in our relationship. Can we talk about this? Do you forgive me?"

Unable in that moment to find a safe way out of the situation, I quickly nodded, trying to disguise my vulnerability with casualness. "Sure," I replied. "It's fine."

This was clearly the response the person wanted to hear. They quickly called others into the room and smiling through tears announced to the gathered group, "Susannah told me she forgives me! Everything is fine now!"

Fine . . . except that the harm done in this relationship had never been acknowledged. Fine . . . except that I wasn't sure what "forgiving" someone whose actions in my life had been so catastrophic would entail. Fine . . . except that I was sure then that forgiveness was, once again, a concept being used to control me. Fine . . . except that the abuse would be repeated on other occasions, and I knew it.

The logic of forgiveness struck me as deeply wrong, but I was unable to figure out what forgiveness was at that time. Instead, that line in the email lodged in my mind (and that line is something I have revisited regularly). At that moment as a young adult, I felt as though I was selfishly choosing myself over long-standing relationships and even my faith—and yet I couldn't force myself to relent from this seemingly un-Christian action.

Though I might not have articulated it then, the God who created me in his image, the Jesus I follow as Lord and Savior, and the Spirit who had led me on my way would not permit me to "forgive" in the way demanded. I knew I felt love for everyone with whom I was setting boundaries. I was not vengeful. I was not trying to cause harm, even though others certainly felt I was sowing discord. All I wanted, all I needed, was for my relationships to reflect that I was a child of God, worthy of safety, dignity, and love. My direct experiences of God didn't seem to line up with the definition of forgiveness I'd internalized from church and my family. Could I really have been so misled?

What I knew I needed to do seemed to be a departure from scriptural tradition. But then again, I didn't know too much about Scripture back then.

Old Testament Forgiveness

Now, the Scriptures are the starting point for me. While many Christian discussions of forgiveness jump straight to the New Testament, the Old Testament holds many gifts for thinking about forgiveness as well. In the Old Testament, passages about forgiveness overwhelmingly emphasize God's agency and capacity to relieve humans of sin. However, divine and human forgiveness are related. Walter Brueggemann writes, "The theological root of forgiveness in the character of YHWH has immense implications for the life of the world. God's willingness to forgive makes possible and authorizes the practice of neighborly forgiveness. Israel will make no cleavage between the love of the God who forgives and the love of neighbor who must be forgiven."[1]

I, like Brueggemann, believe that the human capacity for forgiveness arises from the reality of divine love. But the two are different, and the Old Testament tells us this. The Old Testament canon emphasizes divine grace in the face of human sin. It does not emphasize human grace in the face of abusive power. This is because the Old Testament writers cared so much about justice. The Old Testament prophets do not exhort those whose rights are violated to forgive their oppressors. For example, the enslaved Hebrew people in Egypt are demanded not to remunerate their captors but rather to receive from them precious metals before they depart (Exod. 12:35–36).

The Old Testament stresses forgiveness that chips away at injustice. Sometimes that forgiveness takes an economic form, but it doesn't stop there. An example of this is the forgiveness of debts in the Year of Jubilee (Lev. 25). The primary focus of forgiveness here is making sure that disempowered people don't lose their freedom and autonomy. Forgiveness is the responsibility of those who have power and resources toward the poor and vulnerable. This understanding of forgiveness as addressing social injustice is what is alluded to in the debts/debtors petition in the Lord's Prayer.[2]

Where forgiveness in the Old Testament is concerned, whether forgiveness comes from God or from other people, human repentance precedes it. Significantly, even when God is petitioned to forgive, forgiveness isn't always possible. Even though God is gracious and merciful, sometimes forgiveness remains elusive. In Exodus, God's words to Moses reveal the tension between compassion and the impossibility of full absolution in every instance:

The Lord passed before him, and proclaimed,

> "The Lord, the Lord,
> a God merciful and gracious,
> slow to anger,
> and abounding in steadfast love and faithfulness,
> keeping steadfast love for the thousandth generation,
> forgiving iniquity and transgression and sin,
> yet by no means clearing the guilty,
> but visiting the iniquity of the parents
> upon the children
> and the children's children,
> to the third and the fourth generation." (34:6–7)

If even God's forgiveness has constraints, then the limitations of human forgiveness must be greater.

As Christians, we might be tempted to think that the Old Testament's relatively light emphasis on interpersonal forgiveness reflects a harshness in that part of the canon. We might assume that Jesus came to change all that, overturning the strictures of Old Testament theology and practice with his advent of mercy and love. But this is an unfair and limited reading. To understand Jesus, we have to think of him as a devout Jew for whom the Hebrew Scriptures *were* the Bible. Jesus overturns tables of oppression wherever he finds them, but he never rips out pages of Scripture. He's a teacher who instructs us to encounter the texts afresh. Jesus's forgiveness teachings exist in relationship with Old Testament ones, not in contradiction to them.

Let's examine the nuances of the Hebrew word *nasa'* in relationship to forgiveness. In its most literal translation, *nasa'* means "carry," "lift," or "take," and sometimes, figuratively, "forgive." It's an incredibly common word in the Old Testament, used outside of sin and oppression (e.g., Gen. 13:14;

Exod. 14:16) as well as in situations where sin against God or other humans is concerned (Gen. 50:17; Exod. 32:32; 1 Sam. 25:28). The word *nasa'* appears when a person is burdened with sin as well as when a person decides not to punish another person for their wrongdoing. The word *nasa'* has a highly physical meaning. The weight of sin is not something merely to spiritualize; it presses down on our entire beings.

In Genesis 50:17, when Joseph's brothers address him after realizing that he is the brother they sold into slavery, their petition involves *nasa'*: "I beg you, forgive the crime of your brothers and the wrong they did in harming you. Now therefore please forgive the crime of the servants of the God of your father."

Pharaoh's interaction with Moses in Exodus 10 intertwines interpersonal and divine forgiveness, as Pharaoh, however briefly, recognizes that his oppressive behavior is a violation before Moses and God. Pharaoh first entreats Moses for this forgiveness, believing that he will be able to intercede for him with God. "Pharaoh hurriedly summoned Moses and Aaron and said, 'I have sinned against the LORD your God, and against you. Do forgive [*nasa'*] my sin this once, and pray to the LORD your God that at the least he remove this deadly thing from me'" (Exod. 10:16–17). In this instance, though Exodus doesn't remark on Moses's emotional stance or intellectual perspective, Moses does what Pharaoh asks and goes to pray to God.

In 1 Samuel 25, forgiveness appears rather ironically, as King David wants to act impulsively to kill Nabal and his men because Nabal rudely refuses him hospitality. Though her husband is a fool, Abigail intercedes to protect Nabal and all whose lives depend on him. "Please forgive [*nasa'*] the trespass of your servant, for the LORD will certainly make my lord a sure house, because my lord is fighting the battles of the LORD, and evil shall not be found in you so long as you live" (1 Sam. 25:28). To his credit, David recognizes that the forgiveness here is actually to his own benefit—as incurring bloodguilt for killing a fellow Israelite (even one who is acting like a jackass) wouldn't be productive. Yet even here, the appearance of repentance precedes the forgiveness extended.

In each of these instances, *the petition of the sinner precedes the response of the one who has been wronged.* The one who has done wrong asks for the one wronged to take this action of "lifting" the burden of wrongdoing. The forgiving does not come first. Rather, the person harmed responds to the repentance of the perceived perpetrator.

Viewing interpersonal forgiveness as confidence in God's justice rather than in human retribution, I detect themes of forgiveness in passages even where the usual words don't appear. Esau does not kill Jacob after he steals his birthright and blessing. Ruth continues to seek the wellness of Naomi even after the older woman tries to slough her off like excess weight prior to her journey back to Bethlehem. David repeatedly does not kill Saul when he has reason and means to, even as the rejected king continually seeks David's life.

Throughout the Old Testament, God's people stand at the intersection of justice and mercy. Concerns of exacting punishment and restoring community provide competing poles, and between them life hangs in the balance. Our interpersonal struggles with relationships hang in this balance as well. We too recognize that sometimes mercy is given when it is not deserved and that demands for justice must still be met. We observe the sometimes-competing desires of individuals and communities. We know the tension between unconditional love and reciprocity. In other words, the story of divine-human interaction in the Old Testament raises questions that we have to navigate in interpersonal interactions.

Sometimes divine behavior models what's possible in terms of forgiveness, but we must remember that we're not God. What is possible for God in terms of forgiveness may not be possible for us.

The Old Testament teaches us that forgiveness is less about our choices than we might think it is. Its passages of forgiveness emphasize God's actions rather than human actions. It isn't that human forgiveness is unimportant. But the scope of how God can forgive is so much greater than our own. Ultimately, forgiveness is part of God's character. At the end of the day, distinguishing between right and wrong, guilt and innocence, is God's task, not ours.

The fact that forgiveness is ultimately God's task can both encourage us in our pursuit of forgiveness and perhaps relieve some of the underlying anxieties of our forgiveness journeys. Forgiveness on the interpersonal level, from an Old Testament perspective, does not have anything to do with determining guilt or innocence. God alone is judge. We're not in the business of deciding whether people should be punished for their sins or not. Forgiveness for humans is not wiping the slate clean or turning what was scarlet into white, clean fabric (Isa. 1:18). One of the mistakes (and, ultimately, abuses) of church teachings on forgiveness is the false ascription of this divine activity to the human realm. The Bible never asks us to declare our abusers "clean" in a moral sense from what they have done to us. The record of the past still stands. Genuine forgiveness involves, instead, recognizing that the real onus of judgment rests with God, not on our retribution. At the same time, this concept remedies the impulse to insist that victims deny or minimize their experiences or move on quickly.

As a corrective, the Old Testament gives us a way of dealing with interpersonal sins. It suggests the possibility of practicing boundary-setting forgiveness. In Leviticus 19, God does not speak of forgiveness directly but points toward a forgiveness ethic. The text reads, "You shall not hate in your heart anyone of your kin; you shall reprove your neighbor, or you will incur guilt yourself. You shall not take vengeance or bear a grudge against any of your people, but you shall love your neighbor as yourself: I am the LORD" (vv. 17–18). These verses hold in tension both the need to resist hate and the need to hold neighbors accountable for aberrations of the law. Vengeance is not Israel's to take, Leviticus teaches us. The balancing act between self-love and neighbor love reaches its zenith here. In Hebrew, the preposition translated with the English "as" makes clear that neither self-love nor neighbor love takes precedence. The command of the law is to satisfy *both*. We cannot fully know what it is to love our neighbor without loving ourselves. Biblical forgiveness can't exist without healthy self-love.

The Lord's Prayer

New Testament understandings of forgiveness lean heavily on their Old Testament precedents. For many Christians, the Lord's Prayer is a bedrock for understanding forgiveness. In both Matthew and Luke, the Lord's Prayer appears as part of a sermon—in Matthew, the Sermon on the Mount, and in Luke, the Sermon on the Plain. Many Christians understand these sermons as part of Jesus's core teachings, and so his teaching on forgiveness in them seems particularly weighty. Matthew's prayer goes like this:

> Pray then like this:
>
> > "Our Father in heaven,
> > hallowed be your name.

Your kingdom come,
your will be done,
 on earth as it is in heaven.
Give us this day our daily bread,
and forgive us our debts,
 as we also have forgiven our debtors.
And lead us not into temptation,
 but deliver us from evil." (6:9–13 ESV)

The word translated "forgive" is *aphiemi*, which means "let go" or "release." This may seem well and good, but for abuse survivors like myself, the kicker comes in the verses that follow: "For if you forgive others their trespasses, your heavenly Father will also forgive you, but if you do not forgive others their trespasses, neither will your Father forgive your trespasses" (Matt. 6:14–15 ESV). Improper interpretations of these verses have inflicted harm and enabled Christian abusers to stay in positions of power.

Interestingly, in Luke's rendition of the Lord's Prayer, these troublesome lines do not appear:

Father, hallowed be your name.
Your kingdom come.
Give us each day our daily bread,
and forgive us our sins,
 for we ourselves forgive everyone who is indebted
 to us.
And lead us not into temptation. (11:2–4 ESV)

What follows in Luke is not a discussion of the connection between divine and human forgiveness but instead an exploration of the importance of persistence in prayer.[3] Also, the language is different compared to Matthew. While in Matthew "debts" are being forgiven, in Luke "sins" (*hamartia*) are being forgiven—acts that, so to speak, miss the mark and have a moral connotation.

The differences between Jesus's forgiveness sayings in these two Gospels can help us interpret the potentially troubling verses in Matthew. Use of this passage to keep survivors in abusive relationships is outside the will of God.

Jesus's teaching in Matthew has a collective focus. The prayer is addressed to "*Our* Father." Therefore, putting the pressure to forgive on individuals does not make sense. Additionally, in *The Limits of Forgiveness*, Maria Mayo points out how the forgiveness modeled in the Lord's Prayer is bilateral. Asking for forgiveness and receiving it go together. In other words, if we take the Lord's Prayer in Matthew as the singular authoritative teaching on forgiveness in the New Testament, we still should take care to see that the forgiveness being proposed is a two-way street.[4]

Luke's use of "sins" instead of "debts" points to a theological shift as well. In Matthew, economic relationships provide a vehicle for thinking about forgiveness. A powerful man can forgive the debts of a less powerful person indebted to him. He therefore forgoes the unfair privilege of placing that person in debt slavery. Those who are in positions of power can decide to release the debts of those with less power. Matthew's demand for forgiveness relates to situations of clear and marked differences in power. In these situations, when a powerful person forgives the debts of a less powerful person, their relinquishment of debt collection can reflect the extent to which they're open to receiving God's mercy. God is the ultimate debt collector, but he forgoes his just cause to collect all that he is owed.

It's difficult to imagine Matthew's Jesus turning around and saying to those without power, "Forgive unconditionally those who have put you into slavery." This is not the message he gives to the powerless. To them, he offers the Beatitudes: "Blessed are the poor in spirit, for theirs is the kingdom of heaven. . . . Blessed are the meek, for they will inherit the earth" (Matt. 5:3, 5).

When Luke uses "sins," lacking the reference to social hierarchy, the narrative changes. No longer is the injunction to forgive lest we bypass God's gift of forgiveness. This means we need to be mindful of power differences when talking about forgiveness. Forgiveness by a person of great power is different from forgiveness by a person who is vulnerable to exploitation, as in situations of abuse.

Seventy Times Seven

Many Christians come by their idea of limitless, unconditional forgiveness based on Jesus's teaching in Matthew 18:21–22: "Then Peter came and said to him, 'Lord, if my brother or sister sins against me, how often should I forgive? As many as seven times?' Jesus said to him, 'Not seven times, but, I tell you, seventy-seven [or seventy times seven] times.'" Matthew, ever the knowledgeable reader of the Hebrew Scriptures, may expect his readers to think of this passage from Genesis about vengeful Lamech:

Lamech said to his wives:

"Adah and Zillah, hear my voice;
    you wives of Lamech, listen to what I say:
I have killed a man for wounding me,
    a young man for striking me.
If Cain is avenged sevenfold,
    truly Lamech seventy-sevenfold." (4:23–24)

While Lamech claimed his right to vengeance seventy-seven times over, Jesus points his disciples toward a different way of being in the world, one of extending forgiveness many times beyond what may feel proper.

This teaching is followed by the parable of the unjust slave, wherein a king first forgives the debt of a slave who could not pay. That slave immediately refuses debt forgiveness to a fellow slave who finds himself in the same position. The king punishes the slave who refused to extend to others the forgiveness he received. Jesus warns his followers to beware the wrath of their heavenly Father, who expects divine mercy to be met with human mercy.

But limitless and unconditional forgiveness isn't the point. Though Peter's question was originally about sins, *hamartia*, Jesus tells this parable not in terms of sins but instead in terms of debts, *opheilē*, following Matthew's use of "debts" in the Lord's Prayer. Economic inequality becomes the focus of Jesus's forgiveness discussion, and the major concern that Jesus addresses is differences in power dynamics. First, the king has power over his slave—the power to throw not only the slave but also his wife and children into prison. Then the slave, who is no longer responsible for his debt, sees himself in a position of power over another slave who owes him money. He feels emboldened to grab this slave by the throat and demand payment immediately, but his fellow slave is unable to render payment. So the forgiven slave throws the other slave in prison, prompting the wrath and retracted forgiveness of the king. The failure to forgive the debts of the less powerful triggers divine unforgiveness.

The flow of this story from the seventy-times-seven statement is crucial for our understanding. Jesus wants us to understand what kind of forgiveness he is speaking about when he instructs Peter. We are to forgive the debts that others cannot repay particularly when we are in a position of power over them. We are to exercise the principles of the Old Testament Jubilee, practicing the forgiveness that provides material release to the captives.

This is a beautiful vision of forgiveness with roots deep in God's story. And yet it feels almost too good to be true. Jesus's instruction to refrain from exacting the fullness of what is due comes first to the powerful. This is not the forgiveness that has been preached to me and to other abuse survivors. We are neither the king nor the slave who has been forgiven debts. We are instead the slave who has been seized by the throat, bearing the brunt of demands that we can never fulfill and that threaten to end our lives, sometimes quite literally.

Another key point from the seventy-times-seven passage is that Jesus speaks about the psychological reality that forgiveness is not a one-time decision but an ongoing process. Jesus may be referring not only to forgiving a person who commits the same sin over and over but also to the unfair reality that the same situation requires a person to revisit the difficult emotions and physical realities caused by the sin an equal number of times.

This reading matches what I have found to be true in my life as a trauma survivor. For many years, the greatest fear and pain I experienced flit through my mind with regularity. This is how trauma works. These memories are still in the process of being integrated such that my mind and body don't feel the need to revisit them involuntarily. When one of these memories comes up, I must decide how I will respond. Will I choose anger, fear, or resentment as my response? Or will, somehow, the moment be right for me to forgive? If it is, the decision will not be one and done but one I face every time these memories resurface. I choose forgiveness over and over again, even for the same actions. This is different from limitless forgiveness over and over of repeated sins against me, which would feel impossible.

Gracious Forgiveness

The Gospels teach us that forgiveness between people is reciprocal. However, this is not the New Testament's only model of forgiveness. In Ephesians 4:31–32 and Colossians 3:13, forgiveness arises as a response to the death and resurrection of Jesus.[5] In Ephesians 4:31–32, repentance is *not* mentioned as the prerequisite for forgiveness. Rather, the writer (working in Paul's name) instructs his audience, "Put away from you all bitterness and wrath and anger and wrangling and slander, together with all malice. Be kind to one another, tenderhearted, forgiving one another, as God in Christ has forgiven you." The forgiveness proposed here appears to have both emotional and practical, action-centered components. Emotions such as anger have an important role in the process of forgiveness, even according to the Pauline writings (we'll explore this in chapter 2). These emotions are good, valuable, and even holy, serving as signposts of all that is wrong and ungodly in our world. However, the Pauline writer recognizes that anger and resentment are not the ideal end points of life in Christ.

The vocabulary of forgiveness is quite different here than in Matthew and Luke. The verb translated here as "forgive" is not *aphiemi* but instead *charizomai*. This verb uses the Greek root *charis*, often translated as "grace" or "favor." This type of forgiveness is framed as an extension of grace, which finds its origin in God.

At its root, *charizomai* is a manifestation of divine love. Colossians 2:13 states, "And when you were dead in trespasses and the uncircumcision of your flesh, God made you alive together with him, when he forgave us all our trespasses." Forgiveness here is God's gracious self-expression to humanity, taking place without human initiative. In Romans, Jesus Christ is the ultimate gift of grace: "He who did not withhold his own Son but gave him up for all of us, how will he not with him also give us everything else?" (8:32). Here, used outside the context of forgiveness, *charizomai* indicates the self-giving of God to humanity.

The Colossians 3:13 teaching of forgiveness takes a similar approach. As in Ephesians 4:31–32, the writer does not mention repentance as the prerequisite for forgiveness: "Bear with one another and, if anyone has a complaint against another, forgive each other; just as the Lord has forgiven you, so you also must forgive." Again, *charizomai* is used, and the saving actions of Jesus fuel forgiveness. Independent of this power, we do not and cannot forgive. Interestingly, the New Revised Standard Version updated edition and other translations use "must." However, the Greek doesn't convey the "must": "Just as the Lord has forgiven you, in this way, you also forgive" (my translation). There is no imperative here; forgiveness, when it is present, emanates out of the divine personhood of Jesus.

Luke 7:36–50 shows an interplay between two words for forgiveness. A woman in the house of Simon anoints Jesus's feet with her tears and ointment from an alabaster jar. The Pharisee is offended that this sort of woman is touching Jesus—some prophet he must be! As a corrective, Jesus tells a story of debtors who are relieved of their debts and as a result respond with gratitude: "'A certain creditor had two debtors; one owed five hundred denarii, and the other fifty. When they could not pay, he canceled [*charizomai*] the debts for both of them. Now which of them will love him more?' Simon answered, 'I suppose the one for whom he canceled [*charizomai*] the greater debt.' And Jesus said to him, 'You have judged rightly'" (7:41–43). Notably, neither of these debtors did anything to initiate this forgiveness of debts. They did not, as far as Jesus tells us, beg for mercy, as did the slave in Matthew 18. Thus, the verb *charizomai* seems appropriate: the forgiveness is unilateral and unconditional. It is like the grace of God.

When Jesus shifts from the creditors/debtors story back to the weeping woman, his language changes. Unlike the debtors in the story, the woman *has* shown repentance. She has shown love and kindness to Jesus. Their relationship, at least on some level, is reciprocal. Thus, the type of forgiveness that Jesus offers her is distinctive: he uses *aphiemi* to refer to her. "'Therefore, I tell you, her many sins have been forgiven [*aphiemi*]; hence she has shown great love. But the one to whom little is forgiven [*aphiemi*] loves little.' Then he said to her, 'Your sins are forgiven'" (Luke 7:47–48). The woman washing Jesus's feet with her tears is an active agent in her forgiveness story. On the other hand, the debtors' debts were canceled even though they could do nothing to help their literal redemption. If even those who cannot engage in a reciprocal forgiveness process can be granted mercy, then those who can initiate repentance with love and gratitude are even more included in the kingdom's possibility of forgiveness, no matter their "many sins."

In sum, the New Testament offers us different pictures of what forgiveness looks like. Forgiveness that follows repentance (*aphiemi*) is different from forgiveness that originates only in God's grace (*charizomai*), the kind that is extended in a one-sided way. We may not be empowered to forgive in this way. I'll explore which of these forgiveness possibilities presented itself in my story with Neill as I grappled with the tensions of grace and accountability.

Retaining Sins

In the Gospel of John, the disciples have authority both to offer and to withhold forgiveness. In a resurrection appearance, Jesus gives the Holy Spirit to the disciples and admonishes them: "He showed them his hands and his side. Then the disciples rejoiced when they saw the Lord. Jesus said to them again, 'Peace be with you. As the Father has sent me, so I send you.' When he had said this, he breathed on them and said to them, 'Receive the Holy Spirit. If you forgive the sins of any, they are forgiven them; if you retain the sins of any, they are retained'" (John 20:20–23).

It would be a mistake to read this passage as contrary to the passages explored earlier in this chapter. Nevertheless, these verses correct the idea of universal forgiveness. Here, the word translated as "retain" is the Greek *krateō*, which has a physical sense of holding on or grasping. In this passage, Jesus doesn't mention the condition under which sins are to be retained or grasped. Though repentance appears elsewhere in the Gospels as the determining factor for how to handle forgiveness, here repentance isn't mentioned. Instead, it appears that it is up to the disciples how they will choose to engage anyone who has sinned.

As John stands, some sins can be "retained" without penalty to the unforgiving individual. John's Jesus anticipates that followers will not always choose forgiveness. John 20:23 is the only verse in the Gospel that uses *aphiemi* in conjunction with "sins," and the absence of this pairing elsewhere suggests that this teaching on forgiveness is John's authoritative one on interpersonal forgiveness.

Certainly, this teaching of retaining sins can be used in communities in ways that inflict harm on the vulnerable. This might particularly hinge on how communities understand who exactly is empowered to retain sins. For certain communities, only those who are recognized as having apostolic authority, like the disciples, can retain sins. If these leaders seek to preserve the status quo rather than seek justice, perceived "sins" can lead to unfair punishment and exclusion from the community. In some communities, communal shunning has been a way of retaining sins for unrepentant believers.

Unfortunately, often within the church, those whose "sins" are retained are not perpetrators but instead are survivors, who are seen as wreaking havoc upon community harmony. The "sin" of survivors that communities often retain is the boldness to speak publicly about the abuse they've experienced, to leave their abusers, to participate in arguments with those who hurt them, and to challenge the spotless reputations of those who harmed them. These are not sins.

Jesus is addressing the disciples when he confers this authority to forgive and retain sins, but I believe that the proper extension of this authority is to the entire body of Christians, where "the last will be first, and the first will be last" (Matt. 20:16). In this type of community, survivors—who are surely among the last—receive the safety, justice, and care that put them at the center. What if survivors' ability to retain sins was a legitimate teaching of biblical forgiveness? What would it mean to recognize that Jesus blesses the practice of retaining sins as necessary for the community, even while forgiveness is sometimes necessary as well? It would empower survivors with different ways to respond to their trauma. Those who choose, for whatever reason and in whatever season, to retain sins are not deviating from the way of Jesus but are instead carrying out one part of Jesus's post-resurrection teaching. To be Christlike is not only to forgive but also, at times, to retain sins.

In my experience, though the other biblical passages I've discussed in this chapter have led people to say that I have failed as a Christian, this passage from John has never been cited. I wonder how much of my life would have been different if, in my church communities during my adolescence and young adulthood, there had been those who recognized that retaining sins was as valid a part of Jesus's forgiveness teachings as letting them go.

Jesus on the Cross

As a survivor of interpersonal violence and as a church teacher and pastor who frequently guides others to look at Scripture through a trauma lens, I've thought about Jesus as a survivor.[6] It's been personally significant to me to understand Jesus's identity as Immanuel, "God with us," bearing the depth of human pain. Jesus not only experienced the violence that I and many others have experienced but also transformed it. Even the devastation of abuse could not keep Jesus dead. He is risen, and yet with scars. The trauma changed him and harmed him, and yet new life is possible. If it's possible for Jesus, then it's possible for those of us who have been abused.

This knowledge has comforted me. While I don't wish my trauma on anybody, the knowledge that God in Christ is really with me and not only knows what abuse is like but also offers the possibility of surviving it, transformed, has given me profound hope. As someone who believes that Jesus Christ is God incarnate, I can know that God has never left me to suffer alone and that there is new life ahead.

Ironically, the way Jesus interacts with his abusers while on the cross has been used by church people to harm survivors by keeping them in abusive contexts. In Luke, Jesus engages the idea of forgiveness while on the cross. Deserted by his friends and followers, except for a group of mourning women, Jesus is crucified, sandwiched between two thieves. On the cross, he says, "Father, forgive them, for they do not know what they are doing" (Luke 23:34).

The way I've always heard this text talked about is that Jesus is the perfect example of forgiveness. Even during his torturous death on the cross, Jesus offered his abusers forgiveness. In this perspective, he held no anger toward his abusers. Not an instant passed between the nails piercing Jesus's hands and Jesus's act of forgiveness.

I know Jesus is kinder and more forgiving than I am. However, this interpretation is troubling because of the way it's used to exploit survivors. If we're told to be just like Jesus, and Jesus had no problem forgiving *even while he was being abused*, then those of us who have anger, resentment, or even hatred toward those who hurt us are in trouble. However, what if those emotions of anger serve an important function (as I'll explore in chapter 2)? What if the moment we're being abused is not the right instance to extend forgiveness to those who are hurting us? What if we simply cannot be Christlike, if being Christlike means that we don't hold abusers responsible?

Again, one of my core beliefs is that Jesus is a safe person. I don't believe, even for one minute, that Jesus's bloody agony on the cross represents his desire for us. Jesus came to bring life, not death; the thief is the one who came to kill, and steal, and destroy, while Jesus came to offer life, and life in abundance (John 10:10). If Jesus's words are used to harm his people, then I don't think the problem is Jesus, and I also don't think the problem is the flock. The issue lies instead with the interpreters.

In the passage in Luke, it seems that what Jesus is doing is quite different from what people often claim is happening. Jesus is not addressing his abusers at all. He is not saying to them, "I, Jesus, son of Mary, forgive you! I absolve you of your sins! Just as soon as I come down from this cross, let's go to a banquet together! Hey, wanna be my disciples?" That's not what happens at all. Jesus is instead addressing God directly. He's praying to God, "Father, forgive them, for they do not know what they are doing."

He leaves the ultimate determination up to God whether those who harmed him are forgiven. Forgiveness is the work of God the Father. Jesus relinquishes the task of forgiveness to God instead of burdening himself with it during his time of agony.

Jesus, God incarnate, did *not* find it appropriate in his fleshly existence to extend forgiveness directly to the abusers around him. The lived experiences of abuse and forgiveness do not appear together in Scripture. To be Christlike is to recognize that while abuse is happening, forgiveness is not possible on the part of the victim. Restored community with abusers is not appropriate in the immediate aftermath of violence either.

Defining Forgiveness

The way I've come to understand forgiveness, based on biblical texts and my personal experience, is this: *I forbear personal retribution in order to resolve the pain of my past.* When I say "I forgive you," I mean "I am not seeking punishment for you. The wrong you did to me need not, as far as I am concerned, stand in the way of your growth into well-being and wholeness. When I look at you, I will see you as a child of God, and I will think of you and treat you with grace. To see you and treat you in this way, forgiveness may mean letting you go." This is where I am now after the trauma of my own situation has been mostly resolved.

I recognize that this definition of forgiveness extends beyond what "the Bible says"—strictly speaking—about forgiveness, which, as I hope I've just emphasized, is often two-sided, sometimes communal, and constrained to certain situations. And that's okay with me, honestly. God reveals wisdom incarnationally through lives and bodies, even as he makes wisdom known through Scripture. I fully expect God to continue to make known power, love, and grace through his people today too. The body of Christ continues to receive and reveal God's goodness in the world.

So my experiences, as part of the body, form what I know of forgiveness, even as I quilt these experiences together with the authoritative words of Scripture. The biblical passages we've explored in this chapter are starting points, not ending ones, for me. I'll build on them with other biblical texts that, even though they might not use the Hebrew or Greek words for "forgiveness" as directly, model for me what forgiveness means for God's people. My story and the Bible's story may start to intertwine, as they do for every believer who seeks to continue the incarnational ministry of Jesus.

The Consequences of Toxic Theology

Throughout my experiences navigating abusive relationships, the overwhelming message from both mainline and evangelical Christians has been focused on forgiveness. On the one hand, so many Christians in my life who knew about what was happening in my marriage preached "forgiveness" as the desirable response, which would involve the "healing" of our broken relationship. On the other hand, non-Christians told me to get the hell out and spoke about Neill in unflattering terms that dehumanized him and failed to acknowledge my deep love for him. I related more with the first group, but the wounds I bore from Neill stung whenever the word *forgiveness* was sent in my direction.

If I did not desire to remain in a relationship with my husband, it was an issue of unforgiveness.

If I told him that I was filing for divorce, it was an issue of unforgiveness.

If I felt anger or wanted to hold him accountable or needed to keep talking about the abuse, I wasn't pursuing Christ's peace in my life.

I've always been a person who's confident in her own ideas, values, and beliefs. It's hard to get me to join a bandwagon that I know is deeply wrong. I couldn't fully accept any of these misshapen ideas of forgiveness, but that didn't mean my path was any less difficult. These experiences made for a lonely journey through the traumas of my young adulthood. For a long time, I felt as though I needed to walk the road of complex and troubling relationships alone because the feedback I got was deeply hurtful as I sought to live authentically and faithfully as a Christian.

Allowing first Lucas and Penelope and later another friend, David, in on my journey felt like risky business. I was afraid of losing myself, of degrading that certain and steady voice that always let me know that I mattered, no matter what happened to me. I was afraid of hearing condemnation for the road I had walked to get to the crossroads where I stood. I was afraid of hearing from them, as I'd heard from so many others, that the shambles of my relational life was a product of my failure.

While Penelope and Lucas initially proposed the forgiveness journey to see if Neill and I could continue our marriage relationship, I ultimately needed answers for myself. I wanted to figure out if there was a way to forgive Neill and still maintain what I had always known to be true: that abuse is never acceptable and that I was created in the image of God.

If forgiveness was in place, would it make any difference in the outcome of the marriage? I wanted to know if our history could cease to have a lingering effect on the relationship while continuing to acknowledge that my pain mattered.

Above all, I wanted to know if my Christianity—the thread that connected some of my earliest memories with my emerging adulthood—was inauthentic. No matter what I did, the memories of hurt that I experienced from Neill still burned too hot for me to lay them aside. If I persisted in ending a relationship because of the pain around these memories, would Jesus understand? If I went ahead and did what my gut, unbidden, had been prompting me to do for years, would Jesus forgive me? And some well-repressed part of myself wondered, would I disappoint God even as I let down my children if I failed to stay in my marriage?

When I started my forgiveness work, I did not fully recognize the diversity of perspectives on forgiveness available in the Bible. I thought of Jesus's forgiveness mandates as directives for unilateral, unconditional forgiveness. I had little other material with which to put them in dialogue. I also had the pressure to forgive and move on that I'd received from my churches and my family. As a result, the entire topic of forgiveness terrified me and yet compelled me in my search for the best path forward.

I no longer would approach the forgiveness topic in the way that I did. I now recognize that the complexity of biblical perspectives on forgiveness invites multiple avenues of response, among which forgiveness is one, to harms that have been committed. Though being a good Christian didn't mean all I thought it did, there have been gifts within this process for both Neill and me. To know what these were, I needed to walk the whole journey, and I invite you to bear witness to it with me.

anger

making peace with holy rage

Why I've Struggled

Anger has not always been the easiest emotion for me to get in touch with. I do "sad" with glorious (if short-lived) tears, I'm great at "happy," I can persevere through "irritated," but "angry" hasn't been a place where I've spent a whole lot of time. Though other parts of this story have flowed freely out of my typing fingers, anger gets stuck as I find myself editing and self-censoring my own emotions.

I was raised a White, Southern, Christian woman. I was polite and friendly above all else, because these things, I believed, were respectable and would win me a position in society. On top of that, I was raised in a context where I felt unsafe when adults showed anger. So I tried not to yell, not to scream, not to get out of control. When I was threatened, my trauma response was not to lash out but to "tend and befriend," to work to reestablish relationships wherever I could—in essence, to stay safe. Anger was the enemy, and to act in anger, I believed, was to slide back toward painful parts of my past I'd rather forget.

But my marriage made me angry—really angry. My anger was directed at both Neill and myself. The source of this anger was the breaking of a rule that I had made for myself long ago. The rule was a good one, I think.

Back when I was a child, when I heard screams and slaps and falling furniture or I got caught in the crossfire, I would run down to the basement to hide. There was a full-length mirror there. I remember once, when I was about ten, sprinting down to the basement in fear. I stood in front of that long mirror and studied my reflection closely. My face looked red and puffy from crying. My hair was falling out of a ponytail. I felt scraggly and unwanted.

"Is this it, God?" I said to my reflection in the mirror, or maybe to a divine I couldn't see. "Is this what you think of me? Do you even love me?"

The ten-year-old I was that day believed she heard the voice of God saying back, "You are beloved to me. And you are worth so much more than this."

I was raised a Presbyterian, and we didn't talk about conversion experiences. That wasn't something even remotely in my vocabulary at that time. But looking back on my life, if I had to pinpoint the time I first sensed myself consciously participating in the great narrative of God's salvation story, that day in front of the mirror would be it. From that day on, I knew my worth, and I knew my identity as beloved. Through everything else that happened to me in my childhood and through the difficulties of my young adulthood, I knew that God loved me. And though I'd question many other things, I wouldn't seriously question the reality of God's love or presence.

Based on the knowledge that I was God's beloved, I made myself a rule or, maybe better, a promise, intensely felt even as a ten-year-old child: just as soon as I got into a place of enough power that I could make choices for myself, I would never allow someone I loved to hurt me. I swore that anyone who hurt me physically or emotionally would be *out*. I would not tolerate a relationship in which I was getting hurt. Abuse would always be a line in the sand, and when it was crossed, I told myself, there would be no redrawing that line. I'd end the relationship then and there.

Neill understood my rule. Early in our relationship, I shared with Neill the story of my past and the reality that, for me, there could be no relationship once that line had been crossed. He promised me, "I would never hurt you. I would rather die than hurt you."

I believed him. I had no reason to disbelieve him. I believe even now that Neill meant what he said. In many ways, during our marriage, Neill was my advocate. In time, Neill did not hold to his promise not to hurt me . . . though true to his word, he did flirt with death during the process.

The worst happened in May 2018, about six months after the abuse initially started. I was around twenty-two weeks pregnant with our second daughter. One night, awake at 3:00 a.m. and tired of his refusal to acknowledge the end of our marriage, I flushed my engagement ring and wedding ring down the toilet and told him what I had done. "Hear me," I demanded. "I don't want to be married. I want a divorce."

He took hold of me and shook me hard.

"Please stop," I said. "You're physically assaulting me."

He smiled eerily. "Do you want to find out what it's really like when somebody physically assaults you?"

He pushed me hard against the wall.

I remember screaming and begging, "Please stop! You're going to hurt the baby."

"I don't care!" he screamed. "Nothing matters any more. I'm going to kill myself."

He let me go then—to get knives from the kitchen, it turned out. I ran to the nursery, grabbed our crying toddler, and barricaded the two of us in the bathroom with my phone.

He came after me quickly.

"Get out of there! Don't you dare call for help," he screamed. He punched through the door, and it popped open. I could see he had a knife in his hand. He kept holding it to his throat, hard enough to draw blood. He dragged me out of the bathroom, cutting my hand in the process. He grabbed my phone from my hand.

"If you call the police, I'll run at them and get them to shoot me," he told me.

I believed that he and I were both going to die that night. I had to save our lives, because I couldn't get away. He was stronger and angrier. So I talked to him, cajoled him, and lied to him that I would never tell anyone what he had done, that it could be our secret. I told him I would never leave him. I talked him into a calmer and safer state. I told him whatever I thought he needed to hear to keep us alive.

After episodes like this, I became the angriest I have ever been in my life. I knew that I was worthy of love and safety and that Christ had wagered his own life on that worth. I knew that a real marriage would never include abuse. I knew that my boundaries had been crossed in ways that it would be difficult to recover from. I knew that my power had been taken away and the dynamics of the relationship had changed so that I couldn't view the two of us sharing this life together anymore. I couldn't believe that the future I had always longed for was being torn from me through the actions of a man.

The anger I felt toward Neill became compounded because, through his actions, I encountered even more ongoing harm. I filed a police report after the May 2018 episode in an effort to create a paper trail to gain custody of our children. That triggered Child Protective Services (CPS) to come, which resulted in an outcome I didn't expect. When CPS came in response to that report, and later in response to the trauma surrounding our daughter's birth in September 2018, the workers did not help me or tell me safe places where I could go. Instead, they asked me, "What did you do to make your husband hurt you? Why did you fight with your husband?" They asked me, "Why are you traumatizing your children?" They told me, "We will take away your children if we ever have to come back because we hear a report about your house." They refused to hear the truth that my efforts to leave Neill were actually resulting in his suicide attempts and physical abuse. I was the victim who was blamed. I was the mother who was told that her efforts at parenting were unworthy and destructive. I was the woman traumatized by the threat of having her babies—who were all she had—ripped from her arms. I knew all this was wrong. Though CPS workers never took any action, I believe their involvement left deeper and more-lasting scars on me than any other aspect of the abuse saga, including Neill's actual violence.

Though Neill's violence and instability did summon CPS workers to my doorstep, Neill himself did not cause them to act in these ways. He was mortified to hear how they treated me. Their actions point to patterns of victim blaming and suggest an appalling abuse of survivors within the system itself. However, it was very difficult for me to separate my relationship with Neill from the CPS involvement. Neill's behavior necessitated the intervention of outside entities. If it had not been for his behavior, I would not have faced the trauma associated with the child protection system. I have struggled to hold in tension the victim blaming that went far beyond Neill hurting me and his actions, which exposed me to it.

Neill has often asked me why others who hurt me seemed to receive my forgiveness much more readily than he did. This was manifestly unfair he told me often. Others in my past seemed to escape with impunity from my wrath, while he, it seemed, suffered the brunt of it. This was a valid question. The only answer I could find to give him was that I trusted him more deeply than anyone else. I expected him to be different from the abusers I'd encountered before. Prior to the start of abuse in 2017, I'd had no reason to believe that he would ever physically harm me. We had a relationship, I believed, based on trust and respect. Together we were supposed to build a family that broke harmful generational curses and that healed wounds in each of us. But this is not what happened.

Initially, my anger about the abuse manifested solely in my communication with Neill that I wanted to leave the marriage. However, instead of listening to me, Neill started making escalating suicidal threats and gestures. I could not find a way out that didn't seem to involve the loss of life: his or my own. My anger intensified as well, and as the worst year of my life wore on, I did things that I look back on with regret. In addition to flushing my rings down the toilet, I ripped up every wedding photograph of Neill and me that I had. I wanted to destroy the symbols of our marriage covenant, which, to me, had been destroyed. I shredded a book that represented, to him, his professional work because I felt his actions toward me should disqualify him from this work. I told him a few times that I hated him. I told him on multiple occasions that I would never forgive him. I told him once that his parents would be ashamed of him if they knew the full extent of his actions.

I wish I had allowed my anger to carry me, in those moments, into the real justice of freedom rather than the false justice of retribution. I am sorry for the pain I caused Neill in those moments. Yet my anger did not mean that I deserved the increased abuse that followed. Even flushing a ring down the toilet does not merit homicidal actions. Demanding a divorce, even in anger, does not justify the use of suicidal threats as manipulation. This was not something that Neill, in his own moments of anger, seemed to recognize. I heard him yell, "Look what you made me do!" as he lamented his abusive actions as reactions to my desire to end the relationship.

Because my anger sometimes preceded his physical abuse, it has been difficult for me to make peace with my anger. It's all too easy for me to blame myself for the unfolding of the catastrophic events that almost took my life. It's difficult for me to sit with anger and hold it, to not suppress it or run away from it. And yet I am increasingly able to honor the validity of anger.

My anger was a justified response to the crossing of boundaries and the rejection of what was good and safe for my body and emotions.

My anger was a product of the certain knowledge that the promises Neill had made to me and that I had made to myself had been broken.

My anger was a product of experiencing the double burden of Neill's abuse and the blame for his coercive suicidal threats.

Imagine a 2018 in which someone had looked me in the eyes and—instead of chastising me for saying "hurtful words" to Neill, instead of telling me that my anger was selfish—had said, "Susannah, your anger is telling you something important. I believe what it is telling you. Let's listen to your anger together and see where it leads us." If anyone had done that, I might have suffered far less violence and trauma. If anyone had done that, Neill might not have violated his own values and identity to the extent that he did. If anyone had done that, my anger might have found its peace before I said and did things that I, too, regretted.

But that is not what happened. My anger, born of good and holy impulses to honor the image of God within me, burned hotter and hotter in 2018, determined to let me know that something was deeply wrong. It burned so hot that it almost destroyed me from within. Every night when I tried to sleep, I heard my inner voice speaking: *He betrayed me. He wronged me. I have been unjustly blamed. He has made it so I can never feel safe with him again.* Sleepless night after sleepless night, for many months, I felt the rage of unacknowledged wrong.

All my anger needed was to be heard, to be thanked, and to be satisfied with actions commensurate with its urgency. What I know now is this: I will never again allow anyone to convince me to ignore the voice of my own anger. Not a spouse. Not a friend. Not a pastor. Not a parent.

Biblical Models of Anger

The book of Psalms is one of the places in the Bible that offers us testimony of what human emotions have to say to God. For many people going through times of suffering, they're relatable. The whole gamut of emotions is found there, from defiant hope and joy to deepest despair. Anger is among the emotions voiced in the psalms. At times, people are directly responsible for life's suffering in very concrete ways. If we hold, as we should, that situations of abuse are not victims' faults, then anger toward abusers makes sense. Psalm 137 reflects an extreme anger that is understandable given the conditions of the Babylonian exile. The beginning of the psalm tells about these conditions:

> By the rivers of Babylon—
>> there we sat down, and there we wept
>> when we remembered Zion.
> On the willows there
>> we hung up our harps.
> For there our captors
>> asked us for songs,
> and our tormentors asked for mirth, saying,
>> "Sing us one of the songs of Zion!" (vv. 1–3)

The lament of the psalmist flows straight from displacement, from the pain of losing one's homeland through warfare, and then from having beloved traditions turned into entertainment for one's enemies. I can only imagine the disempowerment that came from such circumstances.

In response to this pain, the psalmist first expresses sorrow. The people have lost a homeland, sacred sites of worship, connection to communal stories. We can appreciate the psalmist's longing, the yearning for a home that no longer exists. When those of us, like me, who have received a high degree of privilege behold emotions of people experiencing oppression, our job is not to control or judge their responses. Empowerment means, in part, that people have the agency to determine how they respond to their abuse. In fact, the psalm shifts markedly toward anger precisely when the oppressors seek to control the actions and responses of the exiles.

The psalmist's anger is not just any anger but anger of retribution, anger of paying back in kind the harm that was done. Anger here is totally valid. And yet the anger burns hot enough that it sits on the edge of danger.

> Remember, O LORD, against the Edomites
> > the day of Jerusalem's fall,
> how they said, "Tear it down! Tear it down!
> > Down to its foundations!"
> O daughter Babylon, you devastator!
> > Happy shall they be who pay you back
> > what you have done to us!
> Happy shall they be who take your little ones
> > and dash them against the rock! (Ps. 137:7–9)

Here it's important to highlight that these are not reports of what the psalmist is actually doing but rather what they are telling God about their feelings. We don't know if the exiled people of God would act on their violent imaginings; we hope they would not. However, the anger at the injustice of exile was important for the psalmist to express before God. Saying to God how absolutely, utterly, and totally incensed we are is acceptable and even holy in God's sight. God's grace and love are sufficient to love us through our most troubling emotions. And while most people we know are probably not the best outlets for the totality of our unfiltered rage, I hope everyone has at least one safe person who can receive those emotions and validate them, mirroring the character of God.

Therefore, our reading of this psalm needs to shift from denunciation to curiosity. What if, instead of turning away from the psalmist's rage, we're able to recognize that these horrific fantasies about infanticide come from an unsatisfied sense of how the world ought to be? The psalms, along with other parts of the Hebrew Bible, reflect the honest struggle of humanity seeking to relate again to God after some of the most painful human experiences. In learning to sit with these experiences, in learning to let the anger exist unfiltered and unedited, we can learn to respect and tend to our own experiences of anger. Anger itself is not the issue. It represents valid and unmet needs.

Anger toward God

A common experience of survivors is to feel angry not only toward the abuser or the abuser's accomplices but also toward God. For many people, the question "Why did God let this happen to me?" is authentic and important. The forgiveness journey, then, is about reorienting oneself not only toward other humans but also toward a God who may no longer feel safe, kind, or powerful.

This kind of struggle with God is woven throughout Scripture. The name of God's people in the Old Testament comes from Jacob, renamed Israel after his epic all-night struggle with the man-angel-God by the Jabbok River. After this encounter, Jacob walks away wounded but also blessed with a new name: Israel—that is, "he struggles with God" (see Gen. 32:28, my translation). Wrestling with God is not a roadblock to faithfulness in the biblical tradition but rather its epitome. Through wrestling with God, Jacob ultimately embraces his identity as the eponymous father of the tribes of Israel.

The prophets experience anger as their divinely given mission leads them into abusive encounters with those unprepared to hear their messages. They get angry with God because God led them there on purpose only to be scorned and belittled and at times threatened with death. Jeremiah reflects this rage. God gives the prophet the mission of prophesying the imminent destruction of Jerusalem by the Babylonians, and this instantly puts Jeremiah on the wrong side of Pashhur, the chief temple officer. Pashhur reacts to Jeremiah's mission abusively: he hits Jeremiah and puts him in stocks in public view for all to mock him (Jer. 20:2). Jeremiah hurls his complaints to God:

> O LORD, you have enticed me,
>   and I was enticed;
> you have overpowered me,
>   and you have prevailed.
> I have become a laughingstock all day long;
>   everyone mocks me.
> For whenever I speak, I must cry out;
>   I must shout, "Violence and destruction!"
> For the word of the LORD has become for me
>   a reproach and derision all day long. (Jer.
>   20:7–8)

Jeremiah is understandably angry. He has been obedient and has told the truth to God's people, but he encounters abuse as part of following God's calling. He has done the best he could for as long as he could, and violence against him is his only reward. He feels as if God duped him into obedience. The promise hasn't been fulfilled, it seems, and Jeremiah experiences abuse from those around him as violence coming from God.

The book of Job is another example of someone feeling abandoned by God in the wake of catastrophe. Job, like so many others, experiences bereavement, loss of his livelihood, and ill health, all in short succession. Job is not, in the Bible's telling of events, "patient" but rather willing to confront the realities of unfairness in his world. He faces not only the hardships of his circumstances but also the hardship of theologies being imposed on him. He faces the accusation that he has done something wrong to deserve his suffering. He encounters the problematic idea that his suffering is supposed to have a pedagogical role. Neither of these concepts are accurate explanations. The witness of the biblical tradition is that sometimes suffering far and away surpasses what is reasonable and just, and that often the most vulnerable people experience the consequences of suffering far more than the powerful, whose decisions are often more damaging.

Job pushes back against these harmful theologies, and rightfully so. It's difficult for him, though, to separate God from these theologies *about* God. In the wake of these harmful theologies, Job isn't sure what can take their place. In his response to God, Job faults God for what he has experienced—if for no other reason than that God has not intervened directly to stop Job's suffering.

While anger is reflected at many points in the book of Job, one peak comes in the following verses:

> He has cast me into the mire,
>   and I have become like dust and ashes.
> I cry to you, and you do not answer me;
>   I stand, and you merely look at me. (30:19–20)

Nonintervention, to Job, is equivalent to active harm, and his perspective makes sense to most people who have experienced abuse at the hands of one person while bystanders observed and did nothing.

To Job, his situation is like having to defend himself in court, where he is representing himself and God is a prosecutor who withholds information about why he is being indicted. Job rages at the silence:

> O that I had one to hear me!
>   (Here is my signature! Let the Almighty answer
>   me!)
>   O that I had the indictment written by my
>   adversary!
> Surely I would carry it on my shoulder;
>   I would bind it on me like a crown;
> I would give him an account of all my steps;
>   like a prince I would approach him. (31:35–37)

God is withholding even Job's right to know what he is being accused of. Job is being held in a dungeon of suffering without the opportunity to justify himself before God.

Ultimately, Job's anger is resolved not through clear answers but through encountering a God who, even though he doesn't tell Job the reasons why he is suffering, confirms that Job has spoken rightly about the mystery of the divine (42:7). God's response restores Job's confidence that even though not everything makes sense, Job can rest with assurance of the reality of the God who holds all creation together.

Job's anger resolves despite the absence of clear answers because the root need that he has in the wake of disaster has been addressed. God has seen him and heard him. This doesn't solve all his problems immediately, but it allows Job to know that God is still at work and is not simply a passive observer. And yet God never chides Job for his anger. If anything, God keeps inviting Job back for continued discussion until Job realizes that he has nothing more to say.

> I know that you can do all things
>   and that no purpose of yours can be thwarted.

"Who is this that hides counsel without knowledge?"
Therefore I have uttered what I did not understand,
 things too wonderful for me that I did not know.
"Hear, and I will speak;
 I will question you, and you declare to me."
I had heard of you by the hearing of the ear,
 but now my eye sees you;
therefore I despise myself
 and repent in dust and ashes. (42:2–6)

Job's response shows that he is now satisfied. He will no longer accept the nihilism of death as the ultimate resolution. It is only through having had the opportunity to express his feelings to God that he reaches a point of peace. God treats him like a dialogue partner worthy of respect; though God does not answer all his questions, he encourages Job to continue asking them, pulling Job back into the conversation when he threatens to withdraw.

Gird up your loins like a man;
 I will question you, and you declare to me.
 (40:7)

There is a place for Job to be angry at God. Job is on a forgiveness journey with God because he perceives divine neglect or even abuse. For me, anger toward God for neglect or even participation in my abusers' activities isn't something I've experienced much. This isn't because I'm particularly holy (I'm definitely not) but because I've come to understand God's presence as a co-suffering and the gifting of resilience for me to survive another day and even to thrive again. God has been with me in unexpected ways in my deepest moments of fear and sorrow, from childhood on, and I have

often identified God's voice as the one that rooted my identity and gave me a fierce will to thrive even when other help
was gone.

However, some of my loved ones go through deep times
of questioning whether God cares at all. They have experienced God as failing as a divine parent and seeking their
harm rather than their good. Struggling through situations
of abuse can bring up the question, "If God is really good
and powerful, why does such harm occur?" For those who
have believed all their lives that God's promises are true
and then suddenly experience what feels like the removal
of that love and grace, the emotional consequences can feel
devastating. God, as much as anyone else, can become one
of the characters in a person's story who is the object of
forgiveness—or not.

For those who seek to forgive God, I think the biblical
witnesses explored here are especially important. Even if
God is the object of our forgiveness journey, anger can be
an important part of the process. It's okay to be mad at
God. The Bible contains many stories of those who are mad
at God. It's an emotion that God is able, willing, and gracious to hold. Anger at God does not make a person a bad
Christian; rather, it makes us humans who have been deeply
committed to believing in a God who makes all things well.

Anger in God's Character

One way that Christians, especially mainline Christians, have
participated in the disempowerment of survivors is by at-
tempting to divest God of the full emotional range of the divine present in Scripture. I know from my own story growing
up that there was a strong pushback against the "angry God"
of the Old Testament, while there was a generous embrace

of the "loving God," especially the one made known in the peacemaker Jesus of the New Testament. This dichotomy is false—God is plenty loving in the Old Testament, and God in Christ is plenty angry in the New Testament. It is also harmful to our Jewish siblings, whose Scripture becomes marginalized, misunderstood, and caricatured. I think the Christian impulse to highlight "positive" stories comes from a good place, recognizing the harm of valorizing divine violence. But at the same time, ignoring that anger is, indeed, part of God's character further marginalizes the already marginalized by suppressing change-making anger. More often than not, ignoring this anger doesn't get rid of it but rather fuels it and bars healthy and empowered expression. My story is an example of this.

In the Bible, we see that God is angry over injustice, particularly abuse of the vulnerable. We, created in God's image, can expect to be angry too. We can experience and process anger without shame, without feeling as though it will twist us into something less than we are created to be.

Ezekiel gives a stark example of God's anger against leaders of Israel because of their unjust interactions with their constituencies. God instructs the prophet to decry the failure of the "shepherds" and promise vindication for the "sheep." God's anger has good cause, one that is outlined at length.

> Thus says the Lord GOD: Woe, you shepherds of Israel who have been feeding yourselves! Should not shepherds feed the sheep? You eat the fat; you clothe yourselves with the wool; you slaughter the fatted calves, but you do not feed the sheep. You have not strengthened the weak; you have not healed the sick; you have not bound up the injured; you have not brought back the strays; you have not sought the lost, but with force and harshness you have ruled them. (Ezek. 34:2–4)

God denounces those entrusted to care for Israel's people for their shameless exploitation. He is angry both for their failure to act—failure to feed, failure to heal, failure to seek out—and for what they have done—ruled selfishly, harshly, and abusively. For these reasons, God's anger seems justified. And for the shepherds, that is bad news. God's anger has consequences. God decries, "Thus says the Lord GOD: I am against the shepherds, and I will hold them accountable for my sheep and put a stop to their feeding the sheep; no longer shall the shepherds feed themselves. I will rescue my sheep from their mouths, so that they may not be food for them" (Ezek. 34:10). I think many of us are uncomfortable with the idea of God being against anyone, but the witness of Scripture tells us that God truly is against those who do harm. God prevents abusers from doing additional harm by removing the vulnerable from their control. God cannot and will not tolerate injustice without consequence.

For those of us who identify with the vulnerability of the flock that Ezekiel describes, God's anger can feel like good news. God's anger can mean that God sees us. God pays attention to our unjust suffering. God's anger means that the shepherds can no longer profit unfairly from the sheep. "I myself will be the shepherd of my sheep, and I will make them lie down, says the Lord GOD. I will seek the lost, and I will bring back the strays, and I will bind up the injured, and I will strengthen the weak, but the fat and the strong I will destroy. I will feed them with justice" (Ezek. 34:15–16). God's anger transforms into justice and care for those who have previously been exploited and neglected. God takes on every role that has been perverted and neglected by the abusive shepherds.

As meek and mild as the Savior is often portrayed in Christian culture, Jesus's anger is recorded in the Gospels. Speaking much like an Old Testament prophet, Jesus calls down woe on those who profit from abusive systems:

> But woe to you who are rich,
>   for you have received your consolation.
> Woe to you who are full now,
>   for you will be hungry.
> Woe to you who are laughing now,
>   for you will mourn and weep.

Woe to you when all speak well of you, for that is how their ancestors treat the false prophets. (Luke 6:24–26)

Again, these words seem harsh and maybe even unsafe to those who can rest content when others suffer or who perhaps are even benefiting from others' oppression. Jesus feels anger about the situation of those who are hungry, who are mourning and weeping. Perhaps we can even imagine Jesus saying something like the following:

> Woe to those who abuse,
>   for you will face accountability.
> Woe to you who minimize and gaslight and
>   control.
> Woe to you when your lies are believed,
>   for that is how my abusers spoke about me.

As wonderfully diverse as the Gospel accounts are, each of them includes what is sometimes called the cleansing of the temple. In this scene, Jesus is furious and acts in ways that we might be uncomfortable with. John's account places this event at the beginning of Jesus's ministry. It's just after the happy occasion of the wedding at Cana.

The Passover of the Jews was near, and Jesus went up to Jerusalem. In the temple he found people selling cattle, sheep, and doves and the money changers seated at their tables. Making a whip of cords, he drove all of them out of the temple, both the sheep and the cattle. He also poured out the coins of the money changers and overturned their tables. He told those who were selling the doves, "Take these things out of here! Stop making my Father's house a marketplace!" His disciples remembered that it was written, "Zeal for your house will consume me." (John 2:13–17)

Jesus's whip is not merely ornamental, and his turning over of the tables is not just a clumsy trip. He is angry that a place that should provide sanctuary is being turned into an opportunity to take advantage of those in God's care. In Mark 3:1–6, Jesus becomes angry when tradition gets in the way of caring for people. On the Sabbath, normally a day of rest, he meets a man with a hand he is unable to use. Of course, Jesus wants to heal the man, even though it's the Sabbath. The authorities around Jesus are already mentally putting him on trial for breaking tradition. Their unwillingness to take seriously the pain of the man before them makes Jesus angry, Mark tells us. If anyone's anger can be regarded as good and holy, it is Jesus's. Jesus models anger as a way for us to speak the truth in love to one another.

What if someone had told Jesus to relax, to calm down, to give it all to God? What if Jesus had been labeled as an angry man and his concerns had been dismissed as invalid because he expressed emotion in ways that were uncomfortable for others? Indeed, some people responded to Jesus in this way. In fact, they crucified him. But the Gospel stories retain the value of Jesus's anger. Because Jesus got angry, exploitation of the poor in the temple courts was challenged. Because

Jesus got angry, a suffering person received relief one day sooner. From the perspectives of those whom Jesus's ministry touched, Jesus's anger brought healing and wholeness.

"Be Angry"

Ephesians contains some of the "household codes" of the New Testament, practical advice for living as Christ followers. At times, reading Ephesians is uncomfortable, given current cultural understandings, for example, of marriage and slavery. We need to be cautious about applying the norms of the ancient world to our current circumstances. But one way in which the advice of Ephesians has been particularly helpful in my own forgiveness journey is in its treatment of anger. It reflects the complex reality of navigating conflict in community, where there's a need for both truth and love. Ephesians 4:25 says, "So then, putting away falsehood, let each of you speak the truth to your neighbor, for we are members of one another." Putting away falsehood includes being real with each other about our anger, all while still loving each other. But sometimes that's difficult.

In my current church context, which is Anabaptist and therefore a peace church, it's easy to jump to the end of the passage, where the Pauline writer encourages the audience, "Put away from you all bitterness and wrath and anger and wrangling and slander, together with all malice, and be kind to one another, tenderhearted, forgiving one another, as God in Christ has forgiven you" (Eph. 4:31–32). Yes, *yes* to all this. But that's not where the passage begins, and we shouldn't start there either. When we encounter anger, either our own or that of somebody else, we shouldn't begin with forgiveness. Anger has something to tell us; it's sometimes the gift that alerts us of wrong in the world.

Ephesians 5 comes just after the writer has finished telling us that walking in the way of Christ means total transformation. We're to take off our old humanity and put on a new humanity, a *kainos anthropos*. The uniform change of our humanity is a dramatic transformation. We put on Christ himself when we follow in his footsteps.

The very first thing the writer talks about after introducing us to the *kainos anthropos*, our new humanity, is anger. It's not a question of *if* we're going to be angry but *when*. And true enough, anger flares often in our lives, sometimes for great reasons and sometimes for not so great reasons. Anger is not inherently bad but rather is a signpost of disruption in our lives, that there has been a rupture of the way we think things ought to be.

Sometimes anger points to a sense of improper entitlement. For example, if I feel angry at one of my kids for embarrassing me by crying in Target, my response to the meltdown speaks much more to my sense of wanting to maintain my public image than to a problem inherent to my kids. My anger isn't inherently bad but an invitation for me to grow as a person and to recognize that people probably aren't judging me as much as I think they are, that meeting my kids' emotional needs is more important than my ego.

But sometimes anger points to something that is desperately wrong in a certain situation and indicates that we are being treated unfairly. In that case, it is not my expectation, leading to the anger, that is the problem but rather the situation itself. In those situations, the challenge is not to take on a more passive, "forgiving" stance but to stretch out my personhood to the fullest extent to address the wrong. Then, indeed, I experience the *kainos anthropos*, the new life into which Christ invites us.

Resolving anger doesn't mean accepting lies or tolerating injustice. As Christians living in community with one another, we are called to honesty, because the truth, as the Gospel of John tells us, will set us free (8:32). Telling the truth to one another, even and especially hard truths, can set us free. We owe it to each other to work through our anger together as we grow.

Ephesians gives us a surprising command: "Be angry but do not sin" (4:26). We are not Jesus, and sometimes our anger spins out of control and inflicts harm even when its origin makes complete sense. "Be angry but do not sin" is actually a quote from the Greek version of Psalm 4. That psalm gives us an idea of how we can have righteous anger without letting it get out of control. The psalm is about asking God for help in the midst of trial. God is the one who hears when we call for help. Anger, dealt with well, involves both attention and release. Notably, attention comes *before* release to God.

> Be angry, and do not sin;
>   ponder in your own hearts on your beds, and be
>   silent. *Selah*
> Offer right sacrifices,
>   and put your trust in the LORD. (Ps. 4:4–5 ESV)

The psalmist tells us to be angry *and*, at the same time, to practice attentiveness. We are to become attuned to what causes anger. We are to rest, removing distractions and getting in touch with ourselves. There is a break, *selah*, between getting attuned to our anger and then offering it to God. There's space to breathe and to be aware of our emotions.

There comes a point when we are fully aware of our anger. We know what it is that we need. At this point, we can turn toward God for satisfaction of all that remains. *After* the anger, we can offer sacrifices—not just of the physical type, perhaps, but also of our anger. We put our trust in the Lord, who, we believe, will make all things right.

We share the psalmist's belief in a God who is both merciful and just, who is working out God's will on the earth. We do not have to go to the point of sin when we are angry, because even if we feel ignored, even if humans disrespect us, God is still attentive to us. God knows the reasons for our anger and takes our pain seriously. God carries our anger alongside us. We are not alone in our anger.

And maybe part of handling anger well means we don't have to carry it forever. Ephesians directs us, "Do not let the sun go down on your anger" (4:26). When I was a child, I thought this meant that if I was still angry at somebody by the time I turned off my light at night, I'd done something wrong. But most commentators take this verse to mean that carrying anger indefinitely isn't wise. Now I understand that resolving anger hastily can be a bad idea. I've learned that I, as an internal processor, usually need time alone during a conflict to figure out my response. Otherwise, I'll usually do or say something I'll regret. But there comes a point when holding on to anger is damaging to us. Anger can replace our experience of love in a way that defines and harms us—even though anger itself is simply a feeling, neither good nor bad. If it becomes the sole, orienting focus of our lives, we can miss out on good things that are waiting for us, including our own justice.

I understand the pull of centering anger. In Bessel van der Kolk's powerful book about trauma, *The Body Keeps the Score*, he writes that certain war veterans he worked with unconsciously held on to their symptoms of trauma so that they would be a "living memorial" to their fallen friends.[1] They believed that if they, in their bodies, weren't holding on to the memories of those they'd lost, their loved ones would be forgotten. And I think we sometimes treat anger like this too. We become living memorials to the injustices we have faced, holding on to anger out of fear that if we don't, the wrongs we've faced will matter to no one. We keep fighting our battles long after we've left the battlefield.

There's good reason to keep moving in our anger journeys, though, and to not let anger become the defining factor of our lives. Ephesians warns us that staying angry too long can "make room for the devil" (4:27). Without careful tending, prolonged and unaddressed anger can invite in the shadows. What began as a right response to wrong can end with the wrong getting in the way of the justice we deserve. And so Ephesians gives us a list of what to *avoid* when we are angry to keep us away from the dominion of sin. Even as we are angry, we are to avoid bitterness, cruel outbursts, and malicious talk (4:31). When we're hurt and mad, all these things are understandable and relatable. At the same time, it's possible to take wrongs seriously, to be angry well, and to practice the way of Jesus. We can resist the wrong, and we can be angry, without our anger harming our inner beings.

Quite simply, anger at the level I felt it in 2018 just isn't sustainable, physically or emotionally. Even though I feel shame for some of the ways I acted toward Neill, I'm glad I could feel the degree of anger that I did, that I could know, right to my core, what I deserved as a person and as a child of God. But there was no way for me to keep carrying that anger. We need to hear the messages that anger sends in order to be safe and healthy enough to do as Ephesians says and move forward in our anger journeys before the sun sets in our lives.

Part of being angry yet not sinning has been, for me, finding ways to hold people accountable for their actions, as I'll discuss in another chapter. Another part of it, as intangible and hopelessly naive as it may sound, is faith. Through my years responding to trauma and abuse, I have trusted that God cares about the wrong that has happened to each of us. This is the same trust that the psalmist expresses when we're urged to "be angry but not sin" before moving into a confession of faith. We can have this trust, Ephesians teaches us, because we know that human interactions matter profoundly to God. Ephesians tells us to take care with the words we use, to speak only what builds up and gives life, because doing otherwise grieves the Holy Spirit (4:30). In other words, wrongful interactions between humans affect God. God is not impassive. God is not indifferent. When we hurt, God cares. We are not alone in the struggle of responding to unjust power dynamics.

The pain we're dealt and the pain we deal matter to God so intimately that it pains the Spirit when one of God's children is wronged (Eph. 4:30). This same Spirit of God infused Jesus's life, and when the Word became flesh and dwelt among us, every pain we have felt, including the pain inflicted through the abusive actions of others, became pain that Jesus experienced on the cross. As a Christian who reads Isaiah through the person of Jesus, I can say with all honesty that I believe,

> Surely he has borne our infirmities
>   and carried our diseases;
> yet we accounted him stricken,
>   struck down by God, and afflicted. (Isa. 53:4)

Immanuel, God with us, the fullness of God, never stands apart from the worst things we experience. He felt the pain of them intimately on the cross. My anger isn't mine alone to carry. And it's in this knowledge that we can safely begin to lay down some of our pain, some of our anger—maybe not all at once but little bit by little bit, maybe so little that we don't even realize what is happening.

Forgiveness can be disorienting. The risk of *not* being mad anymore can be frightening, because it can feel as if we've surrendered our right to justice. But that's not what forgiveness means. The absence of anger and the possibility of peace and joy in its place do not mean that we've surrendered our right to justice or forgotten the wrong. It means that the hurt was so great and our cause so just that we could not resolve them on our own but needed God's intervention. Ultimately—and on no imposed timeline—we can safely surrender our anger to God in the confidence that the Lord defends the vulnerable and upholds the cause of the wronged. Only the justice of God, not the anger we hold, brings the true righteousness we deserve into our lives and into the world.

Books on forgiveness can often dwell on the dangers of anger. Anger, we're told, can make us bitter, twist our character, and turn us into abusers ourselves. When anger is consistently carried to an extreme and remains unprocessed, each of these issues is possible. However, many forgiveness books fail by neglecting how anger is necessary in moving toward forgiveness. Without anger, we bypass full knowledge of what actually needs forgiving. We can miss the opportunity to name and thus address what has harmed us. And for many of us, without anger we might even stay in a damaging relationship or situation indefinitely. This is not what forgiveness is but is rather its antithesis.

Forgiveness entails fully living in and recognizing our anger, attending to the needs to which it points, and then being able to set the remaining anger into the hands of God. Nothing more, nothing less.

From Anger to Justice

Eventually, as the most intense time of the abuse subsided, my anger subsided as well. But it did not dissipate entirely. Flashes of it resurfaced whenever I sensed Neill trying to shift away from the remembrance of those events, in which I always lived. I felt echoes of it every night before I went to sleep (though, blessedly, I could sleep again) and every morning when I woke up, reminding me, *I don't want to be married to him.* As years passed from the most acute periods of abuse, my anger became a quieter companion, waiting, still, for attention and redress.

That occasion seemed to come in December 2020, when parts of Neill's worst behavior emerged again. He again made suicidal threats that seemed intended to keep me in the relationship. After the intensity of this event had passed, I reunited with Neill in Lucas and Penelope's living room. I looked at him, and I felt my anger slowly build. Once again, he had chosen unsafe actions that compromised our family. But this time, unlike back in 2018, I was able to channel my feelings into assertive communication to answer the imperatives of my anger. Lucas was close by to make sure the conversation stayed in safe territory for me. Though my voice shook, I let my anger be heard.

"Neill, I will never allow you to put me in this situation again," I told him. "You have crossed the line too many times."

I was furious, and yet my anger expressed itself not through words or actions I regretted later but through attentiveness to the needs undergirding the anger. Later that week, Neill moved out.

My story is complicated. As I've already shared, after that clear and decisive moment, Neill did come back to live with me again. And again, before long, my anger resurfaced—generally not in overt ways but through a slow simmer that burned in me enough for me to know that something still felt wrong.

It was this shadowy persistence of anger, in part, that Lucas and Penelope responded to when they proposed the forgiveness boot camp. I think they believed that if my anger had a chance to be properly acknowledged and heard, then the marriage could continue. Perhaps anger could morph into forgiveness, and forgiveness could change everything in such a way that the imperatives of my anger would no longer lead to the close of the relationship. I'm grateful to them for hearing my anger and for honoring its validity, for not minimizing the seriousness of the history between Neill and me.

But my anger couldn't just evaporate. It had a message to communicate. What Lucas, Penelope, and I discovered as we walked the forgiveness journey together was that some parts of anger needed to stay for a long time, until the needs to which they pointed were satisfied. Meeting those needs, rather than calming the anger, had to become the focus.

lament

becoming the storyteller again

My Lament

Lament, as described in Scripture, is about naming our losses in the most honest language available to us. It's about putting the losses before God and asking God to intervene for us, or to change our circumstances so that these losses no longer feel so totalizing. I've come to believe that forgiveness is possible only after we've had the opportunity to name our losses. Otherwise, how do we know what or whom we're forgiving?

Forgiveness isn't forgetting; in fact, it requires the deepest kind of memory there is. Lament, for me, is recalling the horrors of what really happened and what was stripped from us and inviting God into that graveyard of loss. Lament allows the type of remembering that makes genuine forgiveness more of a reality.

I find it hard to linger in lament for too long. Most of the time, I am just too busy trying to stay afloat, where I keep jobs with benefits, run a household, and try to be emotionally available to my kids. I'm fortunate, though, to have friends who know me well enough to ask the questions that lead me to stick with the hard things. I think that is what made my times with Penelope and Lucas, as I sat on the sectional in their living room, so powerful for me. Though I could and did tread water most days, they made a space where it was okay for me to feel and name the depth of everything that was wrong. During one session of our forgiveness boot camp, Lucas invited me to lament my losses.

I knew where the losses began, what moments started the chain of events, but I hadn't yet found the place where the losses ended. In a way, lament allows for the reality of loss that is endless, loss that is insurmountable, loss that is nonsensical.

I lamented the following losses in response to Lucas's invitation:

- I lament the loss of innocence that came with the unfolding violence. I am not the person I was, nor will I ever be again.
- I lament the loss of trust in the one to whom I spent countless hours telling everything, once upon a time.
- I lament the loss of home, as the spaces I shared with Neill became unsafe.
- I lament the loss of a dream of a family we would have together.

- I lament the loss of physical health, which emerged in different ways through this process, especially insomnia during the peak of Neill's abuse and the autoimmune diseases that I will have for the rest of my life.
- I lament the loss of sharing happy pregnancy experiences with Neill, and perhaps with any partner.

I offered other laments as well:

- I lament the painful awareness that I often desired to publicly deny our relationship to protect myself from social stigma.
- I lament that I lived through a time when running and hiding from my husband felt like the only reasonable thing to do.
- I lament that I believed I faced the choice of preserving Neill's best interests or staying safe myself.
- I lament that I was in the position of having to emotionally stabilize someone who had just abused me.
- I lament that I often felt alone and stigmatized when I experienced anger, confusion, and trauma.
- I lament the overwhelming moments of fear and pain that I had no choice but to live through.
- I lament the words I heard that tore me apart.
- I lament the ongoing fear I have when I recall our painful history.

There was also much that I lamented for Neill:

- I lament that the journey he walked before he ever met me was deeply painful.

- I lament that he has not felt heard and believed in the ways I have.

- I lament that he learned ways of responding to conflict to keep himself safe that ultimately brought him into danger.

- I lament the constraints of rigid masculinity imposed on him by our culture that meant he could not ask for help when he needed it.

- I lament that I hurt Neill, often unknowingly, through superimposing on him narratives that I didn't know plagued him.

- I lament that Neill committed actions that betrayed not only me but also his own character.

- I lament that after committing these actions he felt cut off from the love and grace of God.

- I lament that Neill's life was so unbearable to him that he often wanted to end it.

- I lament that Neill's mental health crises brought him experiences of injustice.

- I lament that Neill cannot tell the full truth of what he has done and experienced and feel the love and support of those in attendance nevertheless.

- I lament the years of Neill's life lost in shame.

- I lament that my marriage relationship with Neill was so often the source of his identity and sense of worth rather than the fact that God created him in his image and delights in him.

I lamented for my children:

- I lament that domestic violence broke what they knew as a family.
- I lament that my oldest daughter bore witness to many of the worst moments of her parents' lives.
- I lament that I could not give my oldest daughter her expressed longing for a whole relationship between her daddy and me.
- I lament that my middle daughter's entrance into this world was shaped by violence.
- I lament that my middle daughter's biological formation took place while I was so very unwell.
- I lament that my youngest daughter's father could not be present, by my choice, for her birth.
- I lament that my youngest daughter will have no memory of a family in which her father and mother lived together.
- I lament that there have been times when I have been too sad, too angry, or too overwhelmed to be present with them in the way I wanted to be.

My friends waited patiently as I lamented all these things and did not speak until I was finished.

"It seems right to pray now," Lucas said. "Is it okay if we offer all these things to God in prayer?"

The prayer Lucas offered was powerful as he renamed many of the losses and injustices I had identified. He did not sugarcoat them or point out the many ways in which God had already begun to redeem parts of this story. He merely reflected back the pain he had heard in my voice and in my story. He implored God to look and see.

Why We Rarely Lament—and Why We Should

Lament provides a much-needed biblical antidote to toxic positivity in our culture. Toxic positivity is the attitude that, no matter what difficulties we face, the best way forward is with a smile and a dose of denial. The University of Washington's Right as Rain website defines toxic positivity as a way of "dismissing negative emotions and responding to distress with reassurances rather than empathy."[1] This attitude typically comes from discomfort with negative emotions. For example, if I were sharing about my husband's ongoing mental health struggles, someone with toxic positivity might say to me, "Look on the bright side! He's such a good dad."

Toxic positivity ends up hurting victims and survivors. It minimizes their pain and places the burden for their attitude on them. If we are not cheerful, happy, and optimistic, we might become bitter, heaven forbid. But toxic positivity is at odds with forgiveness. If we understand forgiveness as being genuine when it emanates from a recognition of the reality of a situation, then honesty in communication is necessary.

Why do so many people find toxic positivity more appealing than lament? Toxic positivity keeps us in comfort zones where we do not have to attend to the difficult feelings of ourselves or others. It keeps us in a place where we do not have to reckon with the pain of our past. It keeps us in a world where, it seems, human effort and good character can guarantee safety and success.

Christian cultures have often been resistant to lament. Despite the strong presence of lament in the biblical witness, historically, little emphasis has been placed on lament in worship. Its absence, Casey T. Sigmon argues, has major consequences. When all we sing about is the goodness of God, the faithfulness of God, and the blessings we receive, we push away the real struggles of our neighbors and the presence of our own brokenness. Sigmon writes that "recovering lament in worship may re-choreograph the body of Christ out of apathy (which breeds complicity) and into compassion (which generates courage)."[2]

Being able to ignore lament, to pretend that everything is fine or will simply get better, is a marker of privilege. Toxic positivity is not something that many of us who have experienced abuse can access. We have to take into account the darkness. We have to be real about the fact that often things get worse before they get better, if they get better at all. We have to reckon with the fact that sometimes humans choose harm. The world just isn't fair—in a profound, tragic way.

The world of toxic positivity is not where trauma dwells. Trauma shatters the myths that the future is completely in our control, that we can work our way out of anything, that our good character or respectability guarantees our survival. We have tried all the usual methods of survival, and positivity simply isn't adequate. Trauma requires that we reject the language of toxic positivity, which ultimately cheats us through its false promises of security, and that we find hope through a different type of language.

For me, lament has become this language. Lament recognizes that the way to hope is by not denying or avoiding our deepest pain but instead wading through it, with a faith rooted in the fierce realism that God does not, for whatever reason, always stop the deep and stormy waters or the burning fire (Isa. 43:1–3) but that he will be present and attentive when it feels as though we're drowning or being immolated.

Lament in Scripture

Lament permeates Scripture. Though we often think of lament as a topic that occurs with frequency in the psalms, throughout Scripture, lament allows people to respond to the worst situations of their lives, both individually and communally. There are general patterns, such as moving from naming problems to confessing trust in God or praising God. Still, there is a lot of room for improvisation and differentiation even within biblical lament.

Lament can certainly be of different types. Sometimes lament is a dirge that expresses grief over a person who has passed. Sometimes lament is a complaint—not like whining but like laying before God the injustice of a situation in its entirety. Sometimes lament is confessional, as when we recognize our complicity in evil, whether personal or societal, and how our participation in it drags us down deeper into suffering. Some lament in the Bible is deeply personal, from the perspective of an individual. And some lament is communal, in that a whole people group cries out to God about their shared situation.

Lament encompasses many different modes of writing in the Bible. Yet all lament, in essence, brings the starkest experiences of pain, too often pushed into the shadows and ignored, into the light of day—before God and sometimes before a community as well. Lament is the opposite of toxic positivity. Yes, it can lead to a hopeful place, but it does so only by passing through the grime and the muck.

As a Christian, I understand that the basic purpose of my life is to follow the way of Jesus. One core part of Jesus's story, as the Bible tells it, is lament. In Jesus's life, lament bookends the start and the end, particularly in the Gospel of Matthew, the telling of Jesus's life that draws so richly on the patterning of the Hebrew Bible. The massacre of the innocents occurs shortly after the beginning of Jesus's life.

> A voice was heard in Ramah,
>   wailing and loud lamentation,
> Rachel weeping for her children;
>   she refused to be consoled,
> because they are no more. (Matt. 2:18)

Quoting Jeremiah 31:15, this lament is the response to the killing of young boys, one of the most heinous abuses of power documented in Scripture. There is no pressure to move toward forgiveness. There is no exoneration of the ruler. Crying out to God in protest is the natural response. Even though Jeremiah moves toward hope, Matthew does not pressure his listeners to complete Jeremiah's prophecy:

> Thus says the LORD:
> Keep your voice from weeping
>   and your eyes from tears,
> for there is a reward for your work,
>   says the LORD:
>   they shall come back from the land of the enemy;
> there is hope for your future,
>   says the LORD:
>   your children shall come back to their own
>   country. (Jer. 31:16–17)

Lament stands as the children are dead due to Herod's reckless abuse of power.

At the end of Jesus's life, the pattern is similar. As Jesus dies on the cross, his final words reflect the despair of lament without promised restoration: "At three o'clock Jesus cried out with a loud voice, 'Eloi, Eloi, lema sabachthani?'

which means, 'My God, my God, why have you forsaken me?'" (Mark 15:34). This lament, quoting from Psalm 22, is what Matthew (as well as Mark) puts in Jesus's mouth. Jesus experiences utter despair and offers that despair to God, unedited and unfiltered. Even though Psalm 22 includes a confession of trust after the complaint, Matthew does not force these words into Jesus's mouth:

> From the horns of the wild oxen you have rescued
>   me.
> I will tell of your name to my brothers and sisters;
>   in the midst of the congregation I will praise you:
> You who fear the LORD, praise him!
>   All you offspring of Jacob, glorify him;
>   stand in awe of him, all you offspring of Israel!
> For he did not despise or abhor
>   the affliction of the afflicted;
> he did not hide his face from me
>   but heard when I cried to him. (Ps. 22:21–24)

In his Gospel, Matthew recognizes Jesus's final words as lament. Words of praise may yet come, but this is not the time for them. Similarly, when we walk through violence and trauma, these are not the appropriate moments for words of praise to issue from our mouths. The biblical writers wisely know that there is a time for everything.

Lament is interwoven throughout Jesus's life. From cradle to grave, Jesus's existence solicits cries to God, from the mouths of weeping mothers and from his own mouth at the moment of his death. This, to me as a person who has experienced abuse and cried out to God for help, is profound. In lament, we join ourselves to Christ's life, which bears witness to the tragedies of our fallen world.

Both-And

So often in our world and in ourselves we encounter either-or thinking. It would be nice if we could organize everything about our lives into these binaries, but a lot of the time, maybe even most of the time, this isn't fully possible. Especially in difficult situations, like my situation with my husband, the either-or way of thinking simply can't encompass how complicated things really are. I love my husband . . . and he was abusive. I want him in my life . . . and the thought of being near him hurts me.

In moments of loss, whether through a separation, a divorce, or even the death of a loved one who has been abusive, feelings of both-and can seem especially confusing. I take comfort in the fact that in Scripture we see lament bridging the tension. Biblical lament models how to hold together complex emotions.

One of my favorite examples of this comes from the tales of King David: warrior, ruler, adulterer, rapist, and songwriter extraordinaire. When David has already been up to his exploits for quite some time—having defeated Goliath, having sworn his love to Jonathan, and having earned the ire of the first king of Israel, Saul—he finds himself in a place of lament. At this point, Saul has been chasing him all over the countryside trying to kill him, separating him from Jonathan, and denying his legitimacy as ruler even after God's favor has literally been torn from Saul.

After all this, we can imagine that David must be pretty peeved at Saul (although sparing his life multiple times shows David's forbearance!). When David finds out that Saul and Jonathan have been killed in warfare, his response is complicated. On the one hand, this means that David can stop fleeing Saul and establish his own reign. On the other hand,

David acutely feels the loss of Jonathan, whom he loved, and even of Saul, whom, we can imagine, he also (once) loved and respected as a mentor and sovereign. David's lament reflects the complexity of his emotions:

> Your glory, O Israel, lies slain upon your high
>   places!
>   How the mighty have fallen!
> Tell it not in Gath,
>   proclaim it not in the streets of Ashkelon,
> or the daughters of the Philistines will rejoice;
>   the daughters of the uncircumcised will exult.
>
> You mountains of Gilboa,
>   let there be no dew or rain upon you
>   nor bounteous fields!
> For there the shield of the mighty was defiled,
>   the shield of Saul, anointed with oil no more.
>
> From the blood of the slain,
>   from the fat of the mighty,
> the bow of Jonathan did not turn back,
>   nor the sword of Saul return empty.
>
> Saul and Jonathan, beloved and lovely!
>   In life and in death they were not divided;
> they were swifter than eagles,
>   they were stronger than lions.
>
> O daughters of Israel, weep over Saul,
>   who clothed you with crimson, in luxury,
>   who put ornaments of gold on your apparel.
>
> How the mighty have fallen
>   in the midst of the battle!
>
> Jonathan lies slain upon your high places.
>   I am distressed for you, my brother Jonathan;

greatly beloved were you to me;
　　your love to me was wonderful,
　　passing the love of women.

How the mighty have fallen,
　　and the weapons of war perished! (2 Sam.
　　　1:19–27)

Lament can encompass complex emotions without the impulse to explain them away. David can mourn Saul *and* recognize how destructive Saul was in his life. Lament doesn't gloss over the difficult. It doesn't try to skew reactions toward the nostalgic or toward the traumatic but instead recognizes that both can exist.

I deeply relate to this complex lament that David voices. I believe that all he expresses can be genuine. I *know* it can be genuine because I've felt a conflict of emotions too. My husband's violence did not cancel out my love for him, even when I knew, with all my being, how deeply wrong the violence was. My grief for my husband was real, as real, in fact, as my grief for myself.

As I went through trauma over a several-year period, I found that many people around me who knew my story fit pretty well into one camp or another: "Camp Neill Can Do No Wrong" or "Camp Screw That Abuser." Neither camp, ironically, represented my own position. I deeply loved Neill, and I could not forget his abuse. Both were true, and I struggled with feelings of alienation from both camps, as neither, it seemed, really paid attention to the complexity of what I was experiencing. I needed to be able to hold two realities together, to recognize both the love and the pain. I needed to process my experience in a way that honored all of who I was.

Lament did this for me. Following in the footsteps of Hebrew lament, I was able to express what I loved and what I'd lost. I did not have to choose between the two; both were worthy to be offered to God.

God is big enough to hold our complex responses to trauma. God's expanse of love can hold seemingly conflicting realities without the need to reconcile them. God is a witness, a loving presence, who by constant vigil knows what is most deeply wrong. As the psalmist writes, "You have kept count of my tossings; put my tears in your bottle. Are they not in your record?" (Ps. 56:8). God is able to hold all the tears, not erasing the real and needed tensions, leading the psalmist to a place of greater peace. Because God hears, everything feels different. The entire approach to the problem changes.

> Then my enemies will retreat
>   in the day when I call.
>   This I know, that God is for me.
> In God, whose word I praise,
>   in the LORD, whose word I praise,
> in God I trust; I am not afraid.
>   What can a mere mortal do to me? (56:9–11)

Simply knowing that God hears mobilizes the psalmist's turn from despair to praise. The realization that his words fall not to the cold ground but into the loving palms of God's outstretched hands leads the psalmist to renewed hope. Sometimes it takes so seemingly little to change our relationship with our trauma.

Becoming Our Own Storytellers

Lament isn't about acquiescing to victimhood. Lament is one of the most empowering responses to suffering that I know. Rather than tolerating abuse, lament is bold to name it. Lament shines a light on the violence of our world and the anguish that the violence causes. At the same time, lament recognizes that there are situations in our world beyond our ability to fix.

Habakkuk is well-acquainted with this kind of lament. At the very beginning of his book, the prophet lifts a powerful cry to God that conveys how overwhelming the world's wrongs are.

> O Lord, how long shall I cry for help,
>   and you will not listen?
> Or cry to you "Violence!"
>   and you will not save?
> Why do you make me see wrongdoing
>   and look at trouble?
> Destruction and violence are before me;
>   strife and contention arise.
> So the law becomes slack,
>   and justice never prevails.
> For the wicked surround the righteous;
>   therefore judgment comes forth perverted.
>   (1:2–4)

Habakkuk doesn't hold back. He confronts God about the bad things he sees around him. And there are plenty of bad things. Habakkuk lived in a world torn apart by war. He lived sandwiched in time between the aggressive actions of the Assyrian and Babylonian empires. So he asks God hard questions: "How long, God?" "Why all this violence, God?" "Are you really listening, God?" These are questions we might ask God too. Habakkuk models how there's really no limit to what we can say to God within our laments, even at points

accusing God of divine malpractice. In lament, it's okay—
and even encouraged—to name things as we see them.

Lament matters in part because it helps to restore power
to the person who has suffered. Walter Brueggemann writes
about what happens when lament as a speech form disap-
pears: "What happens when appreciation of the lament as a
form of speech and faith is lost, as I think it is largely lost in
contemporary usage? What happens when the speech forms
that redress power have been silenced and eliminated? The
answer, I believe, is that a theological monopoly is reinforced,
docility and submissiveness are engendered, and the outcome
in terms of social justice practice is to reinforce and consoli-
date the political-economic monopoly of the status quo."[3]
Sometimes lament enables us to move from the place of vic-
timization to the place of recovering our role as storytellers.
When Habakkuk laments, one of the answers he receives
from God is that he should continue his prophesying and
tell the story for others.

> Then the LORD answered me and said:
>
>> Write the vision;
>>> make it plain on tablets,
>>> so that a runner may read it.
>> For there is still a vision for the appointed time;
>>> it speaks of the end and does not lie.
>> If it seems to tarry, wait for it;
>>> it will surely come, it will not delay. (2:2–3)

This passage is remarkable. Habakkuk has just spent
verses and verses raising profound theological questions.
And God responds, in essence, "You already know the answers. You already know what you're talking about. Go and
write it!" While being invested with this much authority may

initially be a little unnerving, we can read this divine response as empowering, especially in situations of violence and abuse. We can raise laments to God; this is welcome. We can tell the truth about what we are feeling and experiencing; this is needed. And God empowers us to speak for ourselves to others, to prophetically lead the way for others, even out of our own painful experiences, longings, and questions.

In the biblical narrative, lament is a form of poetic speech that gives power to those historically disenfranchised. This is especially true of women. In the Bible, women are on the margins, frequently objects rather than subjects. Yet lament affords them a unique place of agency. Women are the designated lamenters in many cultures, including ancient Hebrew culture, shaping the words of disenfranchised people to mourn their losses. Consider this passage from Jeremiah:

> Thus says the LORD of hosts:
> Consider and call for the mourning women to come;
>   send for the skilled women to come;
> let them quickly raise a dirge over us,
>   so that our eyes may run down with tears
>   and our eyelids flow with water.
> For a sound of wailing is heard from Zion:
>   "How we are ruined!
>   We are utterly shamed,
> because we have left the land,
>   because they have cast down our dwellings."
> Hear, O women, the word of the LORD,
>   and let your ears receive the word of his mouth;
> teach to your daughters a dirge,
>   and each to her neighbor a lament. (9:17–20)

Women are summoned to accurately give voice to the full sting of dispossession and loss that Jerusalem experiences through her conquest. Women shape how tradition remembers the catastrophe and how it will be passed down. Women, who are to "teach [their] *daughters* a dirge," hold the power to narrate trauma. Those who have been powerless gain, through lament, a foothold in cultural memory.

In the book of Lamentations, we see how those who lament come to have genuine power. This power is something we wouldn't necessarily expect from people who have become victims. However, when people get the chance to express what is on their hearts and minds, everything changes. In Lamentations 1–2, the chief lamenter is none other than the figure of Daughter Zion, the personification of the city of Jerusalem. She is called a queen, and when she speaks, even though she narrates terrible events of cannibalism, rape, and bereavement, people listen up. She is styled as one of the Mesopotamian goddesses of old, and her grief and rage resonate. She has the power to directly address God with pain and outrage.

> Look, O LORD, and consider!
> To whom have you done this?
> Should women eat their offspring,
> the children they have borne?
> Should priest and prophet be killed
> in the sanctuary of the Lord? (Lam. 2:20)

Here, Daughter Zion takes power by flipping the expected narrative on its head. In the throes of abuse, she refuses to shoulder the blame for what happens to her. She instead dares to name those who are actually responsible—from human enemies to, shockingly, the God she believes must have enabled them. Daughter Zion names the wrong that is happening, that women are brought to the point of cannibalism, that religious leaders are being senselessly killed.

Ultimately, this truth-telling lament brings her face-to-face with God. Her role as lamenter makes her powerful.

One way in which lament empowers is through giving us language to name harm. Lament names and heals. It's a difficult and messy process but a restorative one. Casey Sigmon writes, "You know, there is a reason that demons screamed when Jesus passed by: they never like to be named and recognized by the holy one. Lament names the evil and exposes the wounds, so healing can begin. From healing emerges praise that is anything but glurge."[4]

Sigmon expresses that there is power in lament that comes from naming what has held a sinister power. Lament names abuse as abuse. It decreases the power of the darkness while simultaneously summoning the power of the light. Lament does this by daring to bring the darkest parts of our experiences into the presence of God.

From Groans to Praise

In the psalmic form of biblical lament, the poetry very often segues into praise by the end of the psalm. By the end, it seems, the cathartic release of emotions and the sense that God has heard ultimately lead into a celebration of what God has done. In a way, biblical lament models how, in light of the worst experiences our lives have to offer, the way back to praise of God is *through* naming and acknowledging the depth of loss and harm.

In many Christian environments, however, the praise portion of lament is what receives attention. There is a rush to move from the naming of harm to the celebration of goodness. This is not appropriate, especially in circumstances where abuse is involved. Even as we seek to take steps forward from darkness into light, this journey cannot be hurried. It needs to take place at the initiative and desire of the survivor. And this is what Lucas and Penelope did for me. They never pushed me to see the silver lining in any part of my circumstance. They never asked me to praise God through my pain.

And yet in my journey, in spite of myself even, the dark parts of lament have turned to praise. I haven't tried to be joyful. But voicing all the difficult parts has left only gratitude behind in the wake of sorrows. The truth, in my own life and experience, has been that the worst aspects of my marriage couldn't negate the real joy, peace, and even hope I have experienced. Often, that realization comes through time; it is not apparent from the get-go how God's work will unveil itself in our lives, especially through such traumatic experiences as abuse. I have the advantage of retrospect, and it is easier for me to name the faithfulness of God now than it was at the height of the abuse. This has all been part of my forgiveness process.

And so the lament I voiced above feels incomplete without the inclusion of praise. My story isn't complete without describing how God heard and responded to my naming of the hurt. My lament continues not only to name what has gone wrong and what I have lost but also to testify to how God has been active in my life.

- God never abandoned me in the darkest moments of my life.
- God placed within me the resilience to withstand the most horrendous times of the abuse.
- God preserved not only my life but also Neill's life.
- God created in me the capacity to hold together my commitment to my own safety and the safety of my daughters and my love for Neill.

- God brought me friends who loved and supported me, even though it took a while to find out who those people would be for the long haul.
- God restored my ability to sleep.
- God parented me as I have parented my children, and they have grown healthy, happy, and well.
- God has given me a home that feels happy and safe.

And above all else, God has been God. God has been trustworthy. God has been faithful. God has been loving. God has been kind. God has been a vindicator. God has let me know of his love time and time again. God has redeemed my memories so that the slightest reminder of them does not haunt me so severely.

The good things do not cancel out the complaints. The good parts and the mercy of God do not erase how scary, traumatic, unjust, and potentially fatal the hard times were. However, lament models how the two parts stand side by side. Talking about the bad and painful without also talking about the life-giving and holy doesn't feel natural for me. It wasn't that bad things happened in my life for years and then suddenly they stopped and good things started to happen. No, through all the struggle, God was present. God was working. Lament recognizes that the good doesn't supersede the bad but that God strives for the good amid all that's wrong. In a broken and abusive world, lament cries out to God regarding the despair we see around us while also recognizing that God may already be at work in the midst of it. God exists, as the book of Job shows us, even in the trash heap.

Lament isn't a one-and-done phenomenon. It's telling that the writers of Scripture chose not merely to transmit their words orally but also to write them down. Lament is iterative—sometimes we need to do it over and over, even for the same situation. Sometimes the laments of parents are passed down to the children. Sometimes trauma is borne by people removed by decades from the original events creating the trauma. We can't use the presence of praise within lament to argue that somebody's pain is supposed to be over.

From Lament to Forgiveness

A faith that can lament is a faith that maintains hope that God is listening even in the darkest moments. A healing that comes from lament has passed through the worst, most painful parts of memory, and it is authentic. A forgiveness that comes from lament has taken all parts of the story into account.

I believe that forgiveness, true forgiveness, happens only in freedom. It cannot be coerced. It cannot be demanded. It cannot be given from a place of submissiveness or servitude. Forgiveness comes from empowerment. When we are in situations of disempowerment, such as abuse, forgiveness is impossible. Forgiveness, in such cases, can't be given in freedom because a core component of freedom is safety. How, then, can we get to the point of forgiveness after the time of danger has passed and trauma still plays a role in our lives?

Dynamics of power have to change before forgiveness is possible. Lament plants a seed of this change. Lament puts a person, including a traumatized person, in the position of defining reality without minimization or denial, addressing a sympathetic audience (God) to demand redress. Lament also raises the possibility that the harm done through the wrong doesn't have the final say. There may be a point, as we look back, when we realize that God has been active and present. As Brueggemann writes, "Where God's dangerous availability is lost because we fail to carry our part of the difficult conversation, where God's vulnerability and passion are removed from our speech, we are consigned to anxiety and despair and the world as we know it has become absolutized."[5]

When we are empowered by lament, new modes of engaging with trauma become possible. We are now authors of the past and the future. We are conversation partners with God. We have a new place of agency, and from that place we might recognize that the harms of the past are less determinative over our lives than we had believed.

Like Habakkuk, like Daughter Zion, we too, as victims and survivors, gain power through lament, and that power is crucial to forgiveness. Without that power, I'd argue, forgiveness is meaningless, if it even exists. When, through lament, we become real agents once again, free to walk away and free to engage, real forgiveness is on the table. In the authoritative position of one who laments and thus controls the narrative of the story, we are empowered as agents who can make the choice to give or withhold forgiveness.

Certainly there are more practical ways in which power differentials need to be addressed before forgiveness becomes a genuine option. Victims and survivors need the basic power, first and foremost, to secure their physical safety. Differences in how our social systems respond to men and women (which I think my story illustrates) as well as racial-ethnic, socioeconomic, ability, and sexual orientation factors play into how we hold or lack power. I am not arguing that lament takes the place of redress of these factors. However, from an emotional and spiritual perspective, lament plays a role in a sufferer's ability to restore their own power in relating to their own story.

How Lament Changed My Story

Lament helped me to reclaim my power. There had been so little space for me to have agency in my story. My husband had taken away so much of my agency through his actions. I couldn't leave for fear that he'd end his life. I couldn't talk about what had happened for fear of his anger or denial. I couldn't reach out for help for fear of my children being taken away. All of this meant that I was feeling immensely powerless. Lament supplied the language for me to be able to speak about what had happened and regain some sense of control.

The lament prayer Lucas, Penelope, and I prayed that day was cathartic. It was healing because it truthfully named, in a way that perhaps went deeper than a factual recounting of all the details of my story, all the wounds that I carried. It demanded God's notice for a situation so desperately beyond my ability to fix. Speaking those truths about the complex hurt I had experienced in my marriage shifted the forgiveness journey to what had really passed between Neill and me.

Lamenting with Lucas and Penelope felt safe in a way that doing so on my own would not have. Their presence invited me to explore the darkest places of emotion, "the valley of the shadow of death" even (Ps. 23:4 ESV). The Good Shepherd wasn't with us in bodily form, but the participation of my friends showed that I did not carry my fear, anger, sadness, or rage alone. And it has been in some of those deep places of emotion that God has found me, again and again.

Lament implies a deep faith in God, who bears witness and intervenes. It's rooted in the knowledge that God has acted before and can and will act again. So lament, especially as it appears in the psalms, often includes a turn toward a confession of trust, a trust that persists in spite of everything.

But that's a confession of trust I don't have much trouble making. Not through any virtue of my own, my sense of God's faithfulness didn't really waver throughout my experiences of trauma. A gift of my experiences—not native to the experience of trauma itself but rather owing to God's presence, which subverts trauma's power—was hearing God's voice in the midst of my pain.

After the time of lament that I shared with my friends, I found myself in the shower, praying aloud, "God, I can't do this. I can't carry this any longer." My lament, voiced into being the day before, hung heavy in the air around me. I felt that it might suffocate me. In the way that I hear God's voice, not through sound waves but speaking within me, I heard God respond to me, "That's okay. You don't have to carry it. You shouldn't have to carry it. Let me carry it for you." Lament, once again, led me into trust.

Lament didn't change anything about my past situation. It didn't fix my marriage. But it opened me to a reality that the deepest pain I carried could be lifted to God and that this was something I didn't have to do alone; my sister and brother in Christ would support me. As is so often the case in the Bible, individual lament flowed into communal lament. Lament was certainly not the end of the forgiveness journey we walked together, but it was a turning point, a moment when I could begin to envisage all the pain I carried as witnessed by a compassionate presence beyond myself and even beyond my friends.

That moment with Lucas and Penelope certainly wasn't the last time I lamented all that I'd lost. I found that I felt the loss most keenly in the evenings while I did the dishes. I found myself frequently listening to a playlist of my favorite hymns and worship music as I scrubbed the dishes, often crying. As I did the dishes, I thought most of all about the love I had carried for Neill for the better part of a decade, a love that I'd had such great hopes to extend into our family. I offered to God the broken pieces of my life in the audacious hope that something beautiful could emerge from the shards. This time of lament wasn't a painful experience really, but rather a needed time of communion with God in which my tears were an acceptable offering of protest and sadness before the one who could hold them all.

Lament brought the most damaging parts of my experience into the light. The journey could not progress without these truths being spoken and acknowledged in ways I had not done previously. Forgiveness without this lament work would have felt like a farce, built on the mirage of okay-ness that I'd maintained by necessity for so long. I was determined to choose only a forgiveness that could confront the darkest moments of my marriage and scream out their injustice. Yet, rooted in my lifelong faith, I rested also in the confidence that lament's condemnation of evil didn't issue itself vainly and that God bore witness to my cries.

A View from the Other Side of Lament

Today, as I write this story several years after the events initially happened and even a year after the forgiveness boot camp with Lucas and Penelope, some of the things I lament have shifted. Looking back, I can relate to the ways I was feeling on that day, and I can also sense distance.

For a long time, there was little purpose in expressing my pain out loud. It was not safe to do so, and when I would try, my pain fell too often on ears that didn't hear or that minimized. So my survival response became numbness, not actively feeling pain but far from healing. The process of voicing honestly the pain of what happened hurts more at times than suppressing it. Going into the details of that past, I can still at times feel physiological responses to the trauma, and certainly psychological responses of fear, panic, and grief.

And yet I think it's worth it.

Lament means reconnecting with silenced parts of myself. It means building myself back to a place where my body works again. It means actually feeling what was done to me, both by my husband and by the communities that surrounded me.

Through all that, my emotional skeleton regrown, there would come a point in the process where I could forgive my husband. As someone who had agency in how I told my story and related to my pain, I would be able to reach a place where I could *choose* to let that story rest. But prior, without that kind of agency, I would say that forgiveness would have been impossible.

So for me, in my forgiveness journey, lament was crucial to hold together the complexity of my emotions and to restore my role as storyteller. And yet rarely have I heard within church contexts that lament is encouraged for survivors of domestic violence. The pressure to forgive and reconcile is intense, while the invitation to detail, as much or as little as is desired, what has done lasting harm is virtually nonexistent. In the Bible, lament takes up more space than teaching on forgiveness. And yet from contemporary church teaching, I'd have to guess that the ratio is flipped; forgiveness gets far more attention than lament. Ignoring lament cuts us off from our biblical inheritance as well as our path to biblical discipleship. Lament and forgiveness, for me, as a survivor of domestic violence, are inherently intertwined.

Here's a message for the church leaders out there: Don't talk to me about forgiveness unless you've made space for me to lament the full story—the messy parts, the painful parts, the parts I wish I could forget, even the parts I'm grateful for. Don't talk to me about forgiveness until you can sit through my entire lament. If you can't bear to sit and hear the lament, then you probably aren't in a position to tell me what to forgive and what to retain.

Yet forgiveness entails not just feeling or airing the extent of the wrong done to us but also being able to express all pain, sorrow, and anger to the one who can hold it all. Forgiveness means naming what was wrong and why, and feeling that all those events are held by a loving and faithful God.

Lament brings me peace by telling me that God is able to bear with me through the unbearable. Lament is significant not merely because it involves expressing strong emotions in safe ways. It is significant not merely because it names the reality of situations in strong terms. Lament matters because it does all this, and it does so in a way that God is the addressee. Lament takes profound faith, the faith that God is listening to even the deepest cries of our souls.

accountability

*answering for choices and living
with consequences*

The Need for Change

In some Christian models, forgiveness is essentially an absorption of offenses on the part of the victim, with no prior action necessary on the offender's part. Yet when I think about my own situation, this model seems to do more harm than good. For too long I did absorb Neill's offenses, yet that wasn't forgiveness. It was enabling. The more I reflected on my situation, the more I came to understand that accountability, answering for our choices and living with their consequences, affects the course of forgiveness.

The process of forgiveness that the biblical stories model is rooted in accountability (see, e.g., 2 Chron. 7:14). The concept of forgiveness often appears in concert with the concept of repentance, which is a churchy sounding term that I associate with accountability. In Hebrew, it is *teshuvah*, from the Hebrew root *shuv*. *Shuv* connotes a noticeable, tangible turn. A turn from darkness to light. A turn from sin to salvation. A turn from death to life.

Like it or not, we can't make other people turn for us. We can't force *teshuvah* on anybody. And everyone is responsible for their own choices. Moses relays these words to the Israelites in Deuteronomy:

> I call heaven and earth to witness against you today that I have set before you life and death, blessings and curses. Choose life so that you and your descendants may live, loving the LORD your God, obeying him, and holding fast to him; for that means life to you and length of days, so that you may live in the land that the LORD swore to give to your ancestors, to Abraham, to Isaac, and to Jacob. (30:19–20)

I do not mean that we can just make good choices and get ourselves out of any bad situation. I do not mean that genetics, illnesses (including mental illnesses), and other factors of personhood do not shape situations such that we may feel trapped. As one of my brilliant philosophy professors once said, "A choice that I make with a gun to my head is not a real choice."

And yet most people have some degree of control over their responses to situations. We can choose to walk down roads that hint at life or at destruction. We can choose to reach out for help when we need it the most. We can choose to remove ourselves from situations in which we sense ourselves losing control. We can choose to identify and take responsibility for our own emotions and actions.

I wasn't sure how to hold Neill accountable. Neill suffered from severe mental illness, and people told me that I couldn't or shouldn't hold him accountable for his actions: None of what happened was his fault. None of it was something he could control. My insistence on accountability was cruel.

I agree that Neill's abusive behavior occurred while he was experiencing mental illness, which led him into realms he would never otherwise go. In the end, though, I can't say for sure how much he had control over. I guess I'll never know.

But accountability is not punishment. I have never sought to punish Neill. Rather, accountability is an invitation to do what we are created in God's image to do. Holding Neill accountable was not a quest for vengeance but a desire to see him do what I knew was in him: to use the love he carried to repair the family he harmed as much as he was able. Being able to see that good in him was a hint that forgiveness was already underway.

Neill was also responsible to seek and accept help to relieve the symptoms that contributed to his loss of control and ultimately the abuse. He did not consistently take responsibility to seek therapeutic interventions during the height of his abusive behavior. Despite having knowledge of treatments available and many people who would have been willing to help him access treatment, Neill was not open and honest with anyone about how bad things had gotten. He chose to preserve the image of himself that he wanted people to see, and in so doing he hurt me further.

The hard truth that I found myself staring down was this: Neill did not choose to be accountable to me. Not while I was beside him anyway.

The Danger of Asking for Accountability

One of the worst episodes of abuse happened when Neill discovered that I had alerted his family to his behavior. He screamed at me, "How dare you tell them? How dare you tell them anything? I hate you!" Six months pregnant, I scooped up our toddler and ran out of our apartment as quickly as I could. I knew he was coming, and I darted up one of the many staircases in a neighboring apartment building and hid behind a column. My one-year-old daughter and I stared at each other, each of us seemingly asking the other, "How on earth did we get here?"

I let my heart rate slow down, and then I ventured back to our apartment. But Neill was still there getting ready for work, dressed except for his belt.

"This is what happens when you tell anyone what's happened," Neill hissed. "Look at this belt. I'm going to hang myself with it, and you're going to watch. Because you made me do it, because you *told*. Get in the bedroom." He locked me in the bedroom with him and put the belt around his throat.

I don't remember how that situation was resolved, how I managed to pacify him that time. But I do know that afterward Neill sped off to work as if nothing had happened. I was left shaken. What I learned from that episode is that abuse resists accountability. Abuse cannot abide having light shone on it. Neill, at his worst moments, desired both freedom from accountability that would enable abuse and the power to dictate how and whether I told the story. Because of his resistance to accountability, I knew my forgiveness journey required an emphasis on his responsibility for his actions.

The Matthew 18 Principle

In many Christian communities, problem-solving in private is expected. Whether in families or in churches, involving outside scrutiny when there's been abuse is frequently far more controversial than the abuse itself. Abuse often happens within uneven power dynamics. When the systems that enable abuse get called into question, that's scary for people who are part of them and benefit from them, even if they aren't directly abusing others. The victims and survivors who call in outsiders are labeled unloving and unforgiving.

These dynamics figured into my story as well. Neill, my family of origin, and certain church communities expressed discomfort and sometimes outrage over the fact that I wasn't willing or able to keep what happened in our marriage *private*. Each of these individuals and entities was invested in keeping secrets. Shining light on abuse makes the systems that produced the abusers look bad and untrustworthy.

Unfortunately, the roots of some of these attitudes are based in faulty biblical interpretation. Matthew 18 frequently serves as a guidepost for Christian communities. For reasons I'll explain, I'm not in favor of this application in cases of abuse. Here is the passage:

> If your brother or sister sins against you, go and point out the fault when the two of you are alone. If you are listened to, you have regained that one. But if you are not listened to, take one or two others along with you, so that every word may be confirmed by the evidence of two or three witnesses. If the person refuses to listen to them, tell it to the church, and if the offender refuses to listen even to the church, let such a one be to you as a gentile and a tax collector. (vv. 15–17)

"Brother or sister" implies shared leadership and power. Within this situation of mutuality, there's the possibility of a private, internal handling of sins. This isn't the situation in abuse, where power isn't equally shared.

I firmly believe that churches should try to live out Jesus's instructions for being in community. But I also believe that context matters, and I'm sure Jesus wouldn't appreciate his words being used to hurt the very same people he cared deeply about protecting throughout his ministry. Taking Jesus's words about resolving conflicts between equals, in which power is being held equitably and justly, and applying them to situations of abuse puts victims and survivors in danger. What happens when a person tries, on their own, to confront an abuser in a situation of domestic violence? The abuser is even more likely to act out. The abuser will be able to represent the situation of abuse to outsiders however they want by finding ways to minimize and distort the perspective of the person who is actually being harmed.

Pastoral counsel to victims and survivors should not follow the Matthew 18 principle. Pastors and leaders have a responsibility to support genuine accountability. This often can happen only when the victim or survivor is already in a safe place or is being accompanied by people whose power the abuser will respect.

Most of Neill's episodes happened when I tried to seek accountability on my own, which would seem to be consistent with the Matthew 18 principle. He blew up when I tried to talk about his abusive behavior, asked him for a divorce, or sought to get a trusted person from our circle involved. It was my right to do all these things. In practice, I felt as though I was doing what was expected of me as a good wife and Christian. I didn't try to get outside intervention until after he had attempted to kill me.

No one should have to wait that long.

While I have not personally experienced physical or sexual abuse in church contexts (though I have experienced trauma as a result of the response of some within the church who knew about my situation), I know others who have, and the seminary where I taught is marked by abuse as well. When church entities encourage victims and survivors to deal with abusers on their own, without outside accountability, the abuse continues or worsens. Oftentimes, institutions exploit the Matthew 18 principle to justify the ways they willfully failed to protect victims and survivors. They also wrongfully use this teaching to shame victims and survivors who go outside the church for support and advocacy, calling them un-Christian.

In interpreting the Matthew 18 principle, Christians often tend to put the weight on the beginning of the text: that a person who has been wronged by another believer should confront that person individually first. I've already unpacked some of the issues with that interpretation in contexts of abuse. Assuming we could sail past that part of the passage with no red flags, we'd eventually find ourselves at the point of escalated conflict with an unrepentant abuser that calls for kicking them out of the community.

> If the person refuses to listen to them, tell it to the church, and if the offender refuses to listen even to the church, let such a one be to you as a gentile and a tax collector. Truly I tell you, whatever you bind on earth will be bound in heaven, and whatever you loose on earth will be loosed in heaven. (Matt. 18:17–18)

What happened to the kicking offenders out of the church part of the Matthew 18 principle? Why does the person who points out the offender so often get kicked out instead?

Let me be clear. I believe deeply and profoundly in the power of the gospel. This is precisely why I decry the use of Jesus's words to punish victims rather than set them free.

Accountability has a role to play in shaping how forgiveness can authentically happen. Accountability gives us the opportunity to speak the truth in love. If we are not speaking the truth to one another and not holding each other to the best of what we know we are, we can't say that we're loving each other.

Forgiveness doesn't depend on other people's change. We can't determine the choices that any other person in the world makes. This is true even and especially for those who are closest to us. We choose to forgive so that we ourselves can experience more fully the life God wants for us. A desire for accountability opens the door for deeper forgiveness. When we want to hold someone accountable, we are still determined to see the possibility of goodness in them, and that is near the core of forgiveness. The way that accountability unfolds may help to determine what the relationship will look like going forward. When someone is not willing to be held accountable, there is less possibility of continuing the relationship—although, as in my situation, it was difficult for me to conceptualize continuing the relationship even in moments when the offender was accountable.

Reading Matthew 18, we can see Jesus's insistence on getting the relationship between forgiveness and accountability correct. Right after Jesus finishes detailing this process (between equals, in safety), which can end in the expulsion of someone from the community, he launches into the famous seventy-times-seven passage in Matthew 18:21–22. This passage deals not with equals but rather with a king and his servants, and then a debtor and a payee. Forgiveness here allows those who are powerless to have a chance at freedom. It does not counteract the processes of accountability that Jesus detailed previously.

The message I take from this juxtaposition is that forgiveness and accountability aren't mutually exclusive in Jesus's understanding. There are times for each, and there are times when we need to focus on one more than the other. There are occasions when we practice accountability, and even in situations between equals, even when the "brother" is persistent in wrongdoing, even when community restoration isn't possible, maybe there's still a way into forgiveness.

A Glimpse of Accountability

During our separation, while I was pregnant with our third daughter, something new began to happen in Neill. Without the distraction of our relationship and the tug to idolize the bond we shared, he began to experience the love of God for him in new ways, and in that spacious and terrifying wilderness moment, he began to know that his story didn't have to be over. He began to celebrate the truth of 2 Corinthians 5:17: "So if anyone is in Christ, there is a new creation: everything old has passed away; look, new things have come into being!" I saw this happening, in wonder that this kind of growth was possible, and rejoiced that God was doing a new thing in Neill's life.

There was a moment when it seemed possible to hold everything together—my need for his remorse and apology and commitment to continued growth, and his need to be seen in a new light, the light of God. A month after our baby was born, when he had come over to give her a bottle and bond, I broached a conversation with him. I asked him how he saw the events of the past and if there was a way that he could help fill my cup, which could reach the brim only with truth-telling, remembrance, and forgiveness.

He told me: "I hurt you, and I am so sorry. This is no excuse, but I committed those acts in the worst moments of my life, in the worst moments of my insanity. There is nothing that you did to cause those actions, and there's nothing you can do to take them away. They're on me. And since those days, I have done everything in my power to become whole again, God's new creation."

I responded honestly to him: "I don't see you as limited or frozen in time by the worst moments of your life. You are so much more than the worst things you have done. I forgive you. I love you."

I wept in catharsis. It was not my fault. He owned his actions. He understood the hurt he had caused, and without defensiveness, without artifice, and with love, he told me what I needed to hear. It felt as if we had a shared understanding of accountability. In the confidence of a new beginning, I went to our dear friends Lucas and Penelope and told them that, with their blessing, I wanted to start again.

That moment didn't hold. After we were reunited as a couple, I continued to need an ongoing narrative of remorse and remembrance from Neill. He continued to need the affirmation that he was a new creation in Christ, and this meant, for him, disconnection with the past. He was unable to allow me to acknowledge the past without resentment or anger. My need for that ongoing dialogue about the past trauma felt to Neill like a denial of his status as a new creation. We were both hurt. We were both angry. We both felt betrayed.

Over time, Neill's insistence on the irrelevance of the past grew stronger. He would sit in silence or sometimes walk away when I broached the topic of my ongoing pain. All this came to a head about six months after our reunion. I still needed to be heard in my pain, and I let Neill know that this feeling was so strong that I didn't know if I could continue in the relationship. The memories of the past felt so branded in my brain that I couldn't move on.

"But it was not me who did those things!" he angrily replied to me. "It was a different man. *It was not me.*"

"What do you mean?" I retorted. "You have the same name! You look the same! You have the same social security number, the same habits, the same clothes! Someone caused this, someone did this to me, and it sure as heck wasn't me. I know you say you've changed, and I've seen evidence of it, but that doesn't change the fact that *it was you.*"

I think what Neill meant in that moment was that he was *such* a new creation in Christ that the man he was when he abused me was dead and gone. He could not go on with his life, in any healthy way, while holding on to the same identity that he held back then. He was trying to forgive himself in the only way he knew how. But to me, his words were devastating. They undid the healing from months earlier. I wondered if Neill had really meant what he'd said previously or if those words had simply been an insincere effort to restore our marriage.

A couple months after this, Lucas, Penelope, and I were deep into forgiveness boot camp. As part of this process, I had written a detailed narrative of as many events as I could remember, one abuse or effect of abuse per index card. I ended up with sixty-four cards. After I'd written this history down, I felt a need to share it with Neill, to see what he'd say, how he'd respond. I'd never presented him with such a comprehensive account.

"Is this okay to share with Neill, do you think?" I texted Penelope. She hadn't seen the cards yet but had a general idea of their content.

"Just make sure you're ready for his response," she texted back.

These were wise words. It felt as if everything was riding on what he would say or do next. Maybe it was a setup he could never win.

"I have something I want to share with you," I told him. "Is it okay to do that now?" He knew what was coming, it seemed.

"Okay, I guess," he said, sitting on our bed, protectively drawing a pillow up to his chest.

I read the cards to him one by one. All sixty-four. I tried to glance at him while I was reading to gauge his reaction. I read them slowly, deliberately, without adding emotion. Just the facts. All the facts. He avoided eye contact and seemed stoic.

I finished reading. There was silence.

"I guess . . . I kind of wanted to hear your feedback," I prompted him.

He was slow to respond. "I . . . have nothing to say to you. The Spirit is telling me to say nothing. I've got nothing to say."

How could he have nothing to say, I wondered, when I'd poured out my rawest memories to him?

I shared this at my next meeting with Lucas and Penelope after I had done the same thing with them as I'd done with Neill—read the cards slowly, deliberately, and unemotionally.

"He didn't have anything to say," I told them. "He didn't respond. He didn't have anything to offer."

Lucas slowly shook his head. "He didn't respond to what you shared, to what we just heard?"

"No."

"Is it okay if I talk to him?" Lucas asked. "I want to understand what's going on with him, why he didn't respond at all to this. Do I have your permission to talk with him?"

"Okay," I said. "That's fine. I'd like to know if there's anything he could say, because it feels as though everything is riding on this."

A week later, Lucas, Penelope, and I reconvened in their living room, sitting in the same places on their sectional as we had a week before.

"Lucas, did you talk with him? Did you find out if there was anything he had to say, or wanted to say, or thought, or felt?"

Lucas nodded. "I did bring it up with him. He didn't really want to talk about it. Susannah, I'm so sorry. He has nothing to say that will bring healing for you, nothing to say that you need to hear."

I nodded. Lucas's honesty in that moment meant a lot to me. Even as Neill's closest friend and brother in Christ, he didn't try to rescue Neill or make a case that would make me feel differently or reconsider or question the decision I was moving toward.

I'm not sure what accountability looks like in the aftermath of abuse. I'm not sure if a marriage in which someone always has to stare down the worst moments of their life is possible. The deck may have been stacked against Neill. His need to be seen as moving forward from his wrongdoing was valid. He is, truly, more than his worst moments. His life has had meaning and value as a spouse, a father, a professional, a son, a brother, and a friend . . . and, at a more elemental level, it has value because he is created and re-created in God's image.

Neill and I came to be in very different places in the wake of the trauma we'd experienced together. He was the offender, and yet he also experienced traumas. Among these was doing horrible things to someone he deeply loved. I was the victim, and yet I also felt pain over the growing gulf between us. We each needed healing. For me, this was a resolution I sought over and over again in the marriage relationship. I felt as if I needed a thousand apologies, and yet no apology, even when given, sufficed to heal the betrayal I felt. The only way I could move forward was to keep processing, to rehearse the stories over and over, and he was an unwilling listener.

Accountability was too painful for him to tolerate. Neill needed to believe that he was more than the worst things he had done. Neill's actions traumatized him. He did things that were counter to what he and I both knew was true to his personhood, and in the process, he experienced over-whelming dissonance and anguish. To survive, in a physical, spiritual, and emotional sense, Neill needed to distance himself from the abuse. Maybe the word *dissociate* is even appropriate here. He could not experience himself as a person who had performed the abusive actions and go on living.

So often I have heard that I was unforgiving toward my husband, that I prioritized my own wants and needs over his. It's true that I decided, when it was safe to do so, that my personal needs and wants did matter, in spite of how long they had been denied. However, the accountability that I chose moving forward was to hold Neill to the truth of his own humanity: that hurting me and holding me captive through his threats of suicide were as dehumanizing to me as they were to him. I sought accountability not to punish him but to hold him to his divinely given selfhood.

He was not, is not, and never will be a monster. He is a deeply sensitive individual. He is human, and he deserves to be treated as human by everyone he encounters. Sometimes in my anger I failed to treat him as human. That is my re-sponsibility. In his actions, he violated his humanity. That is his responsibility.

I pitied Neill more than I did myself. When I reflected on what had happened, I felt a determination to go on, to overcome, to keep on living, to spit in the face of the evil that is domestic violence. At the end of the day, love of self and love for my children pushed me constantly forward to the next stages of my career, my life, and my relationships. But Neill, tragically, could find no way to love the self he felt he'd become through his actions. He could see no future in light of the pain he'd inflicted upon himself and others. Fortunately, he was able to stay physically safe and gradually became healthier over time, but frozen in our relationship, Neill could not recover from all that had happened.

And yet the deck was also stacked, I think, against me. How was I *not* to ask for recognition of wrongdoing when the primary reminder of that wrongdoing slept with me, ate with me, parented with me? My suffering didn't end when he took his hands off me, when Child Protective Services went away, or when we moved to a different state. Given our previous abuse history, I could not hear his words distancing himself from the abuse as anything but minimization and gaslighting of my experiences.

Rightly or wrongly, my expectation of consistent accountability stymied my forgiveness process. The choice became this: Should I move forward in forgiveness without him, or stay in unforgiveness and continue to need something of him that he could not give me?

Does Accountability Change Anything?

What happens when someone repents or accepts accountability, but it still doesn't resolve the relational rupture? Accountability involves (1) the victim or survivor having the prerogative to decide how and whether the relationship continues, and (2) the offender honoring the validity of their decision, whatever it is. Short of both features of accountability, what an offender is offering is not really a readiness for justice at all but a bandage on the offender's own sense of discomfort.

A recovering offender needs space in which they receive unconditional positive regard, which mental health professionals are trained to offer. They need time to state their feelings without the victim's emotional state taking center stage. But if an offender is genuinely interested in having a relationship with the person they have harmed, the victim has to give consent and set the terms.

As I've said, Neill showed flashes of this kind of accountability. But he was angry and frustrated that I continued to need to talk about what had happened. As it turned out, Neill could not live in a relationship in which what I understand as accountability continued long term. By the same token, forgiveness was not possible for me within that relationship without an openness to that accountability. Even with accountability, though, I wouldn't have wanted the marriage at that point.

However, accountability from Neill was still my right, regardless of what direction I chose to take regarding our marriage. In Neill's case, I don't believe it was fair for him to exhibit accountability temporarily and expect my needs would be met forever in that regard. I don't think it was fair for him to get angry that his accountability didn't get the response he wanted, which was a restoration of our relationship.

Jacob's Accountability

The Bible gives us a window into what accountability could and should mean in light of forgiveness. One of my favorite stories in Scripture is that of Jacob wrestling with the angel. This encounter comes at a crucial moment. Jacob is finally heading toward a family reunion after the break in his relationship with his brother, Esau, after he manipulated Esau out of his birthright and blessing. Esau initially wanted to kill him, but Jacob fled and lived for more than twenty years away from his family unit. He got married, first to Leah, through trickery, and then to Rachel, the favored one. He seems to have recognized, maybe out of his sense of shame, that he needed time to grow up as a person away from those he harmed.

Jacob is on the way back to his home country when he hears that Esau is approaching with four hundred warriors. This doesn't seem like a fortuitous beginning to a forgiveness story; it actually seems as if Esau is about to wipe Jacob and his household and livestock off the map. Messengers deliver this alarming news, to which Jacob responds with defensive measures: "Then Jacob was greatly afraid and distressed; and he divided the people that were with him, and the flocks and herds and camels, into two companies, thinking, 'If Esau comes to the one company and destroys it, then the company that is left will escape'" (Gen. 32:7–8). The narrative doesn't give us a window into Esau's thoughts, but Jacob's motivations seem clear. He's afraid that Esau is coming for a fight. He realizes that the time of reckoning has come. He prays to God while also hedging his bet that God will feel obliged to keep his promise to multiply Jacob's family: "Deliver me, please, from the hand of my brother, from the hand of Esau, for I am afraid of him; he may come and kill us all, the mothers with the children. Yet you have said, 'I will surely do you good, and make your offspring as the sand of the sea, which cannot be counted because of their number'" (32:11–12). Then he sends gifts ahead of him to smooth the road prior to their arrival.

We don't hear Jacob acknowledge what he has done. We don't hear his commitment to change. It seems as though Jacob is doing everything he can to protect himself while also avoiding accountability.

That is, until God intervenes. God answers Jacob's prayer with deliverance, but part of this deliverance is accountability. Deliverance doesn't mean we move past what we have done to harm others. Deliverance means, instead, that all our deeds come to light before the God who is mercy and justice.

It's a gift of grace when God doesn't acquiesce to our desire to maintain the status quo. God's grace invites us into the fullness of what it means to live in the image of God, reflecting light and love no matter what has happened before. And to live in that way, we have to come to terms with our shadows as well.

Jacob doesn't get to simply placate his brother with gifts and pretend that everything is all right. Because it isn't all right, and God, Esau, and even Jacob know that.

That night a "man" (he's identified initially in Hebrew as an *ish*, a "man") comes and wrestles with Jacob all night.

> The same night he got up and took his two wives, his two maids, and his eleven children and crossed the ford of the Jabbok. He took them and sent them across the stream, and everything else that he had. Jacob was left alone, and a man wrestled with him until daybreak. When the man saw that he did not prevail against Jacob, he struck him on the hip socket, and Jacob's hip was put out of joint as he wrestled with him. Then he said, "Let me go, for the day is breaking." But Jacob said, "I will not let you go, unless you bless me." So he said to him, "What is your name?" And he

said, "Jacob." Then the man said, "You shall no longer be called Jacob, but Israel, for you have striven with God and with humans and have prevailed." Then Jacob asked him, "Please tell me your name." But he said, "Why is it that you ask my name?" And there he blessed him. So Jacob called the place Peniel, saying, "For I have seen God face to face, and yet my life is preserved." The sun rose upon him as he passed Penuel, limping because of his hip. Therefore to this day the people of Israel do not eat the thigh muscle that is on the hip socket, because he struck Jacob on the hip socket at the thigh muscle. (Gen. 32:22–32)

Genesis doesn't clarify for us who this man is. We can only imagine Jacob's confusion and fear as this unknown being attacks him. He asks vainly for a name. At the end of the encounter, Jacob walks away changed. Through the man's touch, he gets a limp. In Hebrew, the verb that conveys this kind of touch is not usually used for violent or harmful touch.

In the end, this is an initiation experience for Jacob. He has to experience what it is to be really changed, from his hip to his name. He has to be defined by the constant process of wrestling, not staying the same but ever reaching for more of God. This, to me, is accountability.

Only after this experience of being changed does Jacob get to meet with Esau. Jacob approaches Esau with humility and arranges his family behind him. No longer is he thinking about just his own safety. No longer is he treating the people around him as buffers, as tools. He faces Esau one-on-one, man-to-man.

But Esau ran to meet him and embraced him and fell on his neck and kissed him, and they wept. . . . Esau said, "What do you mean by all this company that I met?" Jacob answered, "To find favor with my lord." But Esau said, "I have enough, my brother; keep what you have for yourself." Jacob said, "No, please; if I find favor with you, then accept my present from my hand; for truly to see your face is like seeing the face of God, since you have received me with such favor. Please accept my gift that is brought to you, because God has dealt graciously with me and because I have everything I want." So he urged him, and he took it. (Gen. 33:4, 8–11)

The pair's interaction drips with their history, their pain, and also the hope of a different present and future, made possible by the path that *Jacob* has walked. They weep as they meet, a sign of their emotional release (I'll talk about release in a subsequent chapter) and the burdened past between them. Jacob, the one who only took, has learned to give. Jacob, the one who masked his true intentions, has learned transparency and authenticity. He has come into accountability, and that makes this reunion possible.

But Esau still gets to choose how he'll respond. Esau has been harmed. He can see that Jacob recognizes this harm in the way that Jacob approaches him with humility. At the end of the day, Esau's generosity of heart allows him to receive Jacob, and he doesn't need the gifts that Jacob offers. However, I am guessing it sure helps Esau to see that Jacob acknowledges the need for reparations.

God's Justice, Long Term

I wish that people who abuse would have to wrestle an angel, or themselves, or *something* before coming face-to-face with the person they harmed. I wish that God would intercept each one before they attempt a homecoming of any kind, overturning the plan or the gifts they offer as appeasement for bad behavior. I wish that God would propose a wrestling match with anyone who wants to persuade their victim to step back into the relationship.

Anyone who would wrestle with God first—with them I'd be willing to entertain the possibility of full embrace. Anyone who is changed so deeply that their very identity quakes and is transformed—with them I might be able to trust more fully.

But so often that simply doesn't happen. One of my biggest questions for God is why we don't often see his justice play out in real time. We don't see wrestling matches that slow the roll of offenders advancing for reunion with their victims. Good people get hurt, and good people die. I was one of the lucky ones. Abusers often do not have to face up to their actions.

Usually, that wrestling moment when God's grace and justice touch a wrongdoer and change everything is elusive. When we ask why it feels as though God's transforming touch does not more often affect those who do harm, we are not alone. Job notices this problem too.

> Why do the wicked live on,
> > reach old age, and grow mighty in power?
> Their children are established in their presence
> > and their offspring before their eyes.
> Their houses are safe from fear,
> > and no rod of God is upon them. . . .
> They say to God, "Leave us alone!
> > We do not desire to know your ways.
> What is the Almighty, that we should serve him?
> > And what profit do we get if we pray to him?"
> Is not their prosperity indeed their own achievement?
> > The plans of the wicked are repugnant to me.
> > (Job 21:7–9, 14–16)

Job, God-fearing man that he is, is understandably confused that while he is being tortured, those who have not accepted any sort of divine accountability are doing just fine. Good things happen to bad people, and bad things—as well as accountability, which isn't actually bad but often can feel that way—don't seem to discriminate either.

We don't know what God is doing in time. But God is working out his goodness in history through events and situations that are far beyond our vision. Maybe beyond anyone's vision. But the full realization of God's justice is there. And so Job declares, in faith, "I know that my Redeemer lives, and that at the last he will stand upon the earth" (Job 19:25). I too believe that God's justice will triumph at last. Our pain will be redeemed. Even if we do not see accountability and justice fulfilled now, they will come—in ways that are far beyond our vision today.

This doesn't mean that we sit and do nothing about injustice. There are many situations in which we need to get human authorities involved to seek justice. Often, though, even when authorities are involved and the criminal justice system plays out, justice isn't done. Often, victims and survivors can leave the police station or courtroom feeling as if their stories were not heard, as if there was not an appropriate response to the ways they were violated and harmed. Even if an offender is incarcerated, this does not necessarily mean that they've taken responsibility for their actions.

Accountability versus Enabling

It's hard for me to come to terms with the fact that I stayed with Neill out of guilt, not wanting him to feel negative emotions, trying to protect his relationship with our daughters, worrying about how he would cope without me.

In doing so, I wasn't actually helping him. I was enabling him.

When I allowed Neill to go on without accountability because it felt like forgiving him, I wish I had known this:

- Neill would not be helped by staying with me.
- He wouldn't grow by staying with me.
- He would continue to act in scary ways.
- He would, in the end, feel more hurt.
- Accountability wasn't being mean; it was asking only what I knew he was capable of as a decent human being and beloved child of God.

I don't know the statistics about abusers who have such profound experiences of transformation that their behavior patterns are permanently and irrevocably changed. I know anecdotal stories of such change and believe them to be real, but, sadly, they're not the norm. Very often, abuse occurs in cycles. Accountability that changes everything permanently is hard to come by. The shame and self-hatred that offenders can experience make it difficult for them to receive the kind of long-term support that would sustain transformation. This is true for Neill, who I believe felt more anger toward himself than I ever felt toward him.

Accountability isn't necessarily enough to rescue a relationship. Increasingly, I came to realize that the trauma the relationship with Neill had brought into my life couldn't be overcome *within that relationship*. It felt hard and unfair to him, but there was just nothing he could do to change the outcome of our relationship after the abuse. Realizing that even Neill's accountability couldn't bring healing helped move me forward. Forgiveness had to come from outside of Neill, outside of me even. If he had been able to sustain the kind of accountability that I needed, it probably still wouldn't have been enough for me to want to save my marriage. Our marriage wasn't what needed saving first. It was my life.

reconciliation

don't think too small

Shortly after I shared with a church and seminary-affiliated leader confidential information about Neill's abuse and our separation, I received an email that read, "We hope, above all else, that you are working on your relationship." My heart rate accelerated as I stared at the screen, reading this email that, unfortunately, had been sent to both Neill and myself. To this person, the disunity in our marriage was something that I could and should "work on," mutually, with Neill. At the seminary where I worked, certain colleagues offered "marriage mentoring" toward the goal of reconciliation as the antidote to our separation.

One day in mid-December, my phone flashed a notification that a trusted member of a church community had texted me. This person was someone who'd heard from a leader about the violence in my marriage. The text said, "_____ explained the situation to me. I do so pray that reconciliation is possible for you!"[1] After I'd moved into my own house, without Neill, I received an email from someone I love deeply. The email urged me to revisit the possibility of reconciliation, to consider the benefits to my daughters and myself of continuing to try to work on the marriage. While the choice was mine, the writer of this email made clear, the possibility of reconciliation was also there because Neill was a man of "godly character." The burden of a divorce was especially mine—I interpreted—to bear. As I read these messages just weeks after Neill's last major episode, they devastated me. They intensified the guilt I already felt.

Reconciliation was a word that had already figured significantly in our marriage. When I first met the man who would become my husband, in the divinity school library, he was very young, with evangelical fervor and a heightened sense of social responsibility—an irresistible combination to the young woman who was there waiting to check out his books. The dream that Neill shared of his vocation was, first and foremost, one of reconciliation. Neill, himself an urban Black man, wanted to work for the reconciliation of White and Black communities, suburban and rural neighborhoods, and church and academy. That was a vision I could endorse. It seemed that our marriage, given our disparate identities, could bring to life this theme of reconciliation.

Even in the aftermath of severe episodes of domestic violence, I still tried to cling to the idea of reconciliation in our marriage. Looking at a wedding photo twenty-four hours after the worst episode of physical violence in our marriage (which happened the day before our third anniversary), I reflected in a journal entry:

> Three years ago, Neill and I promised to love each other for our whole lives.

This has been a brutally hard year. During the painful times, it can be hard to remember that this beautiful moment was real.

But here's what I think: the beauty of a wedding isn't really just about the beginning of a marriage. Its beauty doesn't disallow the brokenness and ugliness that's part of our humanity along the way.

Instead, its beauty is a symbol foretelling what's yet to come in the end, when the one in whose image we're made is more fully reflected in the love we've shared, *when the reconciliation lived out daily in our relationship reflects Christ's reconciliation of the world to God through his death on the cross.*

Today, I'm horrified that I wrote this. What was I doing talking about reconciliation when I was also desperately calling women's shelters and anyone else I could think of who might help me? Did I use the Lord's name in vain to uphold a marriage that was hurting me?

I desperately wanted everything to be okay. I desperately wanted this relationship to be the one that abuse didn't ruin. I hoped that we could still, somehow, have the family I'd always dreamed of having, in which the reconciliation of all things to God was anticipated in the barrier-breaking love between the two of us. I was a poor grad student with a toddler, pregnant with another little one, isolated from family. I have to remind myself, as well as skeptical others, that I was truly trying to do my best with what I had. That I stayed as long as I did is something I intentionally work on forgiving myself for, which I'll discuss more in the next chapter.

Regardless of the reason for my use of the term *reconciliation*, it was deeply rooted in my self-understanding of marriage. When we joined a Mennonite church in Indiana, we were asked what Bible verses were significant to us. I answered with 2 Corinthians 5:18: "All this is from God, who reconciled us to himself through Christ and has given us the ministry of reconciliation." I said to the assembled deacons of the church, "We feel that our ministry as a couple is reconciliation. We want to model reconciliation in our relationship, and we want to share that reconciliation with the world. If we can't be reconciled to each other, then that, we feel, is a poor witness to the reconciliation of Christ."

Yet after the abuse, *reconciliation* became a word at which I recoiled. If you'd asked me about Neill as a friend, a brother, a father, and a professional, I would have had nothing but wonderful things to say. But as far as Neill's role as a husband was concerned, I couldn't justify a similar response. And this felt like a failure of reconciliation. Whenever Penelope and Lucas told me that *if* I wanted to remain married to Neill in the long term, the work of reconciliation would have to be done, I felt an instinctive revulsion. Penelope noticed it first. She told me, "Susannah, I *really* don't think this is going to work. Whenever anyone brings up reconciliation to you, you are completely repelled. It's like something is attacking you."

Responding to Spiritual Abuse

When I think about the responses I received from other Christians in the wake of my separation from Neill, I feel angry. I feel angry that my wishes and autonomy were not as important as the abstract ideal of reconciliation. Though not all these individuals knew that domestic violence was involved, some did know and chose to prioritize the continuation of the marriage anyway. I believe these responses constitute spiritual abuse. At the point when I finally separated from and divorced Neill, my fellow Christians' responses were more harmful to my emotional well-being than Neill was.

Rather than hastening to forgive these wrongs from my former spiritual community, I'm trying to take a bit of my own advice in this book: I'm sitting with the anger, lamenting what I've lost, and exploring what accountability may come. Because I do not want to go back to the church I attended during this period and do not feel safe having contact with certain individuals, I do not think that reconciliation is likely. I have come to believe that a relationship with the denomination as a whole is unhealthy for me, as I see patterns in how I was treated that are mirrored in the experiences of many other survivors.

Theology can be just as damaging and potentially fatal as a hurled slur or a blow. The communities where I lived, worked, and worshiped had an embedded theology of reconciliation that played out to mean that no matter what I'd been through, it was less important than reconciling with my husband and staying in my marriage. The message conveyed was that speaking up and getting help to leave the traumatic relationship were unkind and even violent actions, but staying in a marriage where I had physically gotten hurt and emotionally been imprisoned was part of God's peace. Reconciliation was a facade that shielded community members from confronting conflict.

Often, when people experience religious trauma, the pressure is on them to stay and change the situation from within. This is not emotional labor that survivors should have to do. I do not lend my voice to change the institutions that were willing to sacrifice my life in favor of a false reconciliation. It is most appropriate for those still in these communities who have not been harmed to do the work of fixing the broken system.

There were resonances of some aspects of forgiveness boot camp with the reconciliation pressure of my church and work communities. Penelope and Lucas initiated forgiveness boot camp with a belief that I might be able to forgive Neill while in the relationship. They also hoped, I believe, that forgiveness might lead to reconciliation. But unlike others in my community, Lucas and Penelope grew with me. They listened. They learned, with me, that the depth of hurt in my marriage meant that forgiveness wasn't possible within it. They released me from hopes that I could not meet.

Reconciliation: God's Work

Since those traumatic experiences in my religious communities, I have explored what the Bible means by reconciliation, both how it is related to forgiveness and how it is separate from it. I wanted to find a way of looking at reconciliation that didn't hurt people who'd experienced abuse. In the Bible, the word translated as "reconciliation" is a lot less common than the words we've explored for forgiveness. The Greek *katallas-*, especially as Paul uses it, shows us that reconciliation originates with God, not with us.

> But more than that, we even boast in God through our Lord Jesus Christ, through whom we have now received reconciliation. (Rom. 5:11)

> For if their rejection is the reconciliation of the world, what will their acceptance be but life from the dead! (Rom. 11:15)

> All this is from God, who reconciled us to himself through Christ and has given us the ministry of reconciliation; that is, in Christ God was reconciling the world to himself, not

counting their trespasses against them, and entrusting the message of reconciliation to us. (2 Cor. 5:18–19)

The primary focus of reconciliation is reorienting the world to God. It also sums up the essence of Christ's headship over the world.

For in him all the fullness of God was pleased to dwell, and through him God was pleased to reconcile to himself all things, whether on earth or in heaven, by making peace through the blood of his cross. (Col. 1:19–20)

Again, the emphasis of reconciliation is who Jesus is and what he does.

R. P. Martin states, "God has achieved a final reconciliation of the world but men and women need to learn to live with moral sensitivity and vigilance until the end comes."[2] Of course, God's actions have implications for humans, who, in Christ, need to embody God's reconciliation. In Ephesians, the Pauline writer indicates how Christ's death on the cross is what has broken down the barriers between Jews and Gentiles.

[Christ has set about] abolishing the law with its commandments and ordinances, that he might create in himself one new humanity in place of the two, thus making peace, and might reconcile both to God in one body through the cross, thus putting to death that hostility through it. So he came and proclaimed peace to you who were far off and peace to those who were near, for through him both of us have access in one Spirit to the Father. (2:15–18)

Again, Christ is the initiator and we are the participants.

There's a bit of bad news, at least for me. In Paul's writing, one example of reconciliation does occur in the context of marriage:

> To the married I give this command—not I but the Lord—
> that the wife should not separate from her husband (but
> if she does separate, let her remain unmarried or else be
> reconciled to her husband) and that the husband should not
> divorce his wife. (1 Cor. 7:10–11)

There's definitely a lot in this verse that could be unpacked, particularly concerning remarriage, but for now, we can take Paul at face value. According to H. Merkel, the language of reconciliation here echoes Hellenistic marriage documents that use the term to reflect the resumption of the marriage relationship after a period of separation.[3] Here, the term *reconciliation* refers to this continuation of marriage after separation. The reference is specifically to a rejoining of two married people, but reconciliation in the Bible also goes far beyond this legal process. To view a divorce as a sign that reconciliation is not at work is wrongheaded. Humans didn't start reconciliation, and our actions don't end reconciliation either. There's a much bigger picture of reconciliation at play that extends beyond marriage. It isn't that humans have nothing to do with reconciliation, but at our best, we're participants, not its initiators. According to 2 Corinthians 5:19, we have been entrusted the message of reconciliation. Being entrusted with this message doesn't mean that the work of reconciliation is ours. Rather, we're the heralds of what God is doing in the world.

In the Hebrew of the Old Testament, there's not an easy one-to-one correspondence between any words and the English "reconciliation." This isn't to say that interpersonal reconciliation or reconciliation between God and people isn't present thematically in the Old Testament, but it does take a bit of work to identify it. There are examples in the Old Testament in which forgiveness appears to have taken place but full reconciliation or restoration of the relationship has not. Take, for instance, the story of Jacob and Esau from Genesis that we've already explored. Even after the very moving scene of forgiveness, Jacob and Esau still go their separate ways: "So Esau returned that day on his way to Seir. But Jacob journeyed to Succoth and built himself a house and made booths for his cattle; therefore the place is called Succoth" (Gen. 33:16–17). From there, the story follows Jacob, not Esau. Esau is the consummate forgiving brother who can see the face of God in his formerly offending brother Jacob's face (Gen. 33:10). Yet the relationship will not be the same in spite of forgiveness.

From this biblical material, I believe that we Christians have vastly overstated the relationship between forgiveness and reconciliation. Forgiveness can definitely be part of reconciliation, but the absence of reconciliation doesn't mean the absence of forgiveness.

When Reconciliation Feels Hopeless: 2 Samuel 14

The church often places the burden of reconciliation on those who have been harmed as the necessary fruit of forgiveness. But reducing reconciliation to something that humans—particularly abused people who are carrying the burden alone—can accomplish makes reconciliation far too small. Reconciliation is the work of God. We as humans can take part in it, but sometimes there's irreparable harm to relationships. Sometimes reconciliation needs to happen at an eschatological level—that is, when the fullness of

God is seen by all people. God can change things in ways we cannot.

I love the story of 2 Samuel 14, one of the finest illustrations of how deep God's passion for reconciliation goes. The Bible's stories are as complicated as our own, especially the story of King David's family. Absalom, David's son, is a devoted brother who seeks to avenge his sister, Tamar, whom Amnon, their half brother, raped. Absalom is angry that David has not held Amnon accountable for the rape, as Amnon is David's favorite son. So Absalom murders Amnon, then flees for his life. The king's nephew, Joab, also the commander in chief of David's army, wants to see Absalom restored into David's good graces for reasons of his own. But Joab doesn't feel as though he can petition David to restore Absalom. So Joab conscripts a woman to fool David into seeing the error of his ways and accepting Absalom back. The woman is to disguise herself as a widow and spin a false tale for the king. It's disappointing that this woman isn't named, so I'll go ahead and call her Mother Tekoa.

The story that Joab concocts and that Mother Tekoa repeats goes like this: Her two sons were fighting, and one killed the other. By law, the murderous brother is now to be killed by the "avenger of blood," the next of kin of the dead man. But allowing this retribution would deprive this already vulnerable widow of *both* her sons. If the woman stands in the way of her son's execution, then *she* could be liable to receive the punishment of death. So-called justice, retributive justice, makes everyone poorer, more endangered.

The point of this story is to get David to realize the flaw in his own retribution against Absalom. If he could extend mercy to the widow's condemned son, couldn't he show mercy to his own? Couldn't Absalom come home again? Joab's scheme works, and David agrees to let Absalom return. This happens even though David eventually sees through the ruse, asking the woman if Joab put her up to the task.

At first glance, we might wonder if Mother Tekoa is merely a minor character. After all, we are told that Joab puts the words in her mouth. But that's not the whole story, for two reasons. First, the woman is called wise. Wisdom in ancient Hebrew literature suggests a special awareness of the world, an understanding of how things really are. It can also suggest a practical agency, the know-how to get things done. Finally, it can suggest an insight into the nature of God and humanity.

Knowing all that, I don't believe that the wise woman is just a puppet of Joab in the story. Joab could have picked anybody to talk to King David. The fact that she is wise must have had something to do with his selection.

Second, a portion of the woman's speech is different from the rest. For the most part, it seems as though she is acting the role of the widowed, bereaved mother that Joab assigned to her. But then there's a profound moment when she seemingly interrupts the script handed to her. In that moment, her wisdom, her deep understanding of the nature of God and the ways of the world, is revealed. Here is what she says: "We must all die; we are like water spilled on the ground, which cannot be gathered up. But God will not take away a life; he will devise plans so as not to keep an outcast banished forever from his presence" (2 Sam. 14:14).

God will not take away a life. That's not a message we normally associate with the Old Testament. We're so accustomed to thinking about God's wrath and judgment in the Old Testament that we're inclined to overlook the moments of mercy and grace within it. The witness of Mother Tekoa is that in God's incredible goodness, justice and mercy become intertwined. Even when we think, like David, that no restoration is possible, that nothing good can come, that a person is no longer capable of carrying God's light and love, God is not done. God keeps searching for ways to bring the outcast back home, to restore relationship, and to mend what is shattered. Mother Tekoa's words are far more than the political machinations of Joab, who has his own agenda for wanting Absalom restored. These are prophetic words of witness to the nature of God, coming not from Joab but straight from God's heart.

Mother Tekoa bears witness to the justice and mercy of God. I want to fully honor her voice in its own right, and yet I'm struck by how closely the message of this woman aligns with what will become the message of Jesus Christ's restorative love in the New Testament. When he's on the cross dying between two thieves, Jesus communicates the persistence of God's love. While one thief mocks Jesus, the Gospel writer tells us that the other thief expresses shame about his actions, remarking that he is justly condemned. Jesus does not deny the condemnation but instead tells him, "Today you will be with me in paradise" (Luke 23:43). The relentless pursuit of God's love weaves its way through the great salvation story that passes through Mother Tekoa, countless other saints of our faith, and ultimately Jesus.

That good news of God's persistent and restoring love is the message that resounds in Paul's words in Romans 8:38–39: "For I am convinced that neither death, nor life, nor angels, nor rulers, nor things present, nor things to come, nor powers, nor height, nor depth, nor anything else in all creation will be able to separate us from the love of

God in Christ Jesus our Lord." The scandalous truth of the gospel, spoken through Mother Tekoa in 2 Samuel, is that God hasn't given up on people even when *we've* given up on them. God's mercy, God's justice, God's passion for shalom are never limited by our constraints. What we deem screwed-up people or screwed-up situations are God's workshop for hope and transformation. As beloved children of this God, we, like wise Mother Tekoa, are called to keep speaking the truth that God's reconciling work isn't finished.

Sometimes that witness isn't enough to change the outcome. Mother Tekoa's story compels King David to bring Absalom back to the city, but he doesn't go into his father's presence for years. Ultimately, the fault lines in the relationship between Absalom and David are so deep that the two permanently part and are at war. Absalom will die in the war, unreconciled to David.

Mother Tekoa's witness matters even in Absalom's death, even though the restoration she sought didn't fully manifest. Her witness points to the foolishness of the cross, the foolishness of love resisting retributive violence, drawing in outcasts. God, Mother Tekoa tells us, does not take away a life. God keeps trying to make a way to bring everyone back home. That's *God's* work, far beyond our efforts and abilities.

In stories where what we consider reconciliation is beyond our capacity, we don't need to feel as if we have failed. I don't believe that God, who is gracious even to our enemies, desires us to be so hard on ourselves. Reconciliation means more than hurt feelings being smoothed over and everyone being happy. Reconciliation means closing the gulfs that separate us—human from human, God from human. Putting bandages on wounds too soon doesn't repair these gulfs but simply denies that they are there.

Christ takes down the dividing wall between us (Eph. 2:14). Christ ultimately makes us one. Christ's work isn't limited to what we can reasonably accomplish in our lives, nor is it limited to the human institution of marriage.

When Knowing and Doing Are Two Different Things

I wish I had understood more about this biblical material back when I was in agony over what to do about my marriage. I felt as though my church background and my personal wishes were completely at odds, and I didn't know what to do about it. On the one hand, the matter felt simple: divorce Neill and get my freedom. On the other hand, the matter felt very complex: ending the marriage would be a failure of reconciliation. Breaking the vows I made at the altar would convey that I cared more about myself than Neill, my children, or the will of God.

Honestly, what I wanted most deeply was in fact godly: to bring everybody, especially Neill, to a place where everyone and everything were safe and all right. But what this looked like for Neill and me seemed different. I thought Neill was best off when I could help him and he could live full-time with our girls, while I felt safest alone. I struggled because I was torn between what I wanted for myself and what I wanted for Neill, and I felt emotional and even physical pain as I tried to bring those two things together.

This crisis peaked one evening in San Antonio, Texas. I was there for a work conference and was staying in a hotel self-proclaimed as the most haunted in the city, as if I needed a few more ghosts to add to the ones dwelling in my psyche. I was traveling with just a non-crawling, frequently napping baby and felt a degree of freedom from the usual chaos with all three of my young children. The second I carted all the luggage into my hotel room and got settled in, I felt things I hadn't experienced in months, not since Neill had moved back in: freedom, peace, rest, the ability to be in a space and not feel like I had to run away.

This feeling of liberation confused me. I loved Neill. Our life together seemed to make sense. We were doing well with money, enjoying time together after the kids went to bed, and planning shared conference presentations. I wanted to please my friends who had invested so much in our relationship. I wanted my girls to have a dad who lived at home with them. I wanted the trauma to be over for me. But there I was in Texas, feeling real wellness for the first time in months.

I strapped the baby into a carrier on my chest and left the hotel to go for a walk. The hotel was next door to the Alamo, hallowed ground for Texans, where a small group of soldiers had taken a tragic final stand against Santa Anna. In the dusk, twinkling lights on the trees gave a magical, otherworldly aura to the paths. Lovers and gaggles of teenagers walked around the grounds, so I was not alone, but I felt separated from everyone else by the trauma I carried.

Walking in the gardens, I knew who I was looking for, but she still took me by surprise when I found her: Susannah Dickinson, in her statue form at least. The survivor of the Alamo sent to tell the rest of the Texan army about the fate of the others. I was named after her. My mom, who lived in Dallas, Texas, at the time of my birth, discovered the name Susannah in a picture book about the Alamo and thought it was the most beautiful name she'd ever heard. Without ascribing a particular significance to the name other than that, my parents linked me to this woman whose statue I now stood in front of.

I don't think Mennonites have official saints, especially not ones who pray as intermediaries for the faithful, but that day she was mine.

Somehow it hadn't registered before that Susannah of the Alamo, like me, was a mother. In her representation outside the Alamo, she is holding a small child in her arms and poised as if on the run. All she could do was take her baby, leave, and bear witness to the reality that something terrible had happened. If no one else could understand me, I thought, Susannah of the Alamo could.

"Susannah," I whispered self-consciously, "please tell me what to do. I'm confused. I'm lost. I need you to help me."

As I said, Mennonites typically don't ask saints for intercession. I hadn't ever. And this statue of Susannah represented no beatified saint that I knew of, just an ordinary woman, like me, who had seen her world crumble around her.

I'm not sure what part of me, what spirit, or what figment of my imagination answered back, but what I heard in my being was this: "It's okay to just survive. It's okay to take the babies, run, and live."

The next morning I found myself afraid. I felt as though I had an answer but lacked the theological means to make any sense of it or carry it through. I was embarrassed to slink back to Lucas and Penelope and tell them that I knew for sure what I wanted to do, that the vows they had heard me make, re-make, months earlier were null and void.

As the baby napped back at the hotel, I pulled out my phone and texted a friend from work, David. David is a fellow PhD, a theologian who pastors a small church in

South Bend, Indiana. His seminary office was two doors down the hall from mine at the time. Earlier that year, David and I had co-taught a course for the first time, to be repeated in subsequent years, where he brought his theological expertise and I brought my biblical studies knowledge. David's role as a pastor, though, was the sphere in which he first earned my trust. David invited me to preach to his congregation at a crucial moment when his church was leaving its denomination and joining another over an important issue of justice. During that service, preaching about how reconciliation doesn't always turn out the way we hope, I was surprised to look up from my sermon and see David weeping, which was out of character for him. After the service, David invited me to stay and listen in on a congregational meeting, during which I learned for the first time more about why David's church was leaving its denomination.

It was an issue that struck close to home. The church's denomination had, in recent years, adopted an official position to oppose divorce even in cases of domestic violence. David and his co-pastor at the time knew that they could not in good conscience accept this stance, both on theological and ethical grounds, having borne witness to congregants' journeys out of abusive marriages. With their congregation and the guidance of the Holy Spirit, they discerned what their next step should be, which entailed leaving the denomination. The church risked the loss of its building, which had become a hub of food and supply distribution in the neighborhood in addition to being a place of worship. Additionally, the denomination could strip David and his co-pastor of their ministry credentials, revoking the blessing for ministry placed on them at the time of their ordinations.

As I heard parts of that story in the congregational meeting and later at the table of David and his spouse, I felt a new sense of trust growing. Many people talk about justice in the name of the gospel, but David was living it out. I could see how David was willing to leverage and abandon his own privilege as a White man to stand in solidarity with survivors of trauma like myself. As I heard David share the story of what he and his congregation were walking through, Matthew 5:10–12 came strongly and unbidden to mind: "Blessed are those who are persecuted for the sake of righteousness, for theirs is the kingdom of heaven. Blessed are you when people revile you and persecute you and utter all kinds of evil against you falsely on my account. Rejoice and be glad, for your reward is great in heaven, for in the same way they persecuted the prophets who were before you." David's willingness to see the injustice of abuse and walk away from the denominational recognition of his vocation meant that he was a safe person. The fact that he didn't know Neill and was in no way invested in my marriage helped too. But David hadn't known much about my situation prior. He'd hoped and assumed, I think, that everything was going well in my family.

And so David was the person I texted the next morning after the Alamo revelation. It was a Sunday morning, and a text from a random colleague traveling in Texas probably was not what he was hoping to see after wrapping up worship in Indiana.

"I'm in trouble," I wrote.

David texted back immediately. "What's up?"

I explained the story as best as I could through text. I then expressed the crucial issue that was on my mind: "I feel like I SHOULD be able to reconcile with him. I mean, he's repented, right? There's nothing else that can be done.

But this hasn't been okay for me, not even for one day. Why can't I reconcile with him?"

I think David's well-chosen next words might have saved my life. "I suspect it has something to do with the ways that our bodies process trauma," he texted back. "It's not your fault that you can't go back to how things were, and you wouldn't be the first person I've pastorally encountered to divorce largely over trauma history (if I'm hearing you right, and this is mainly historical)."

Reading those words in San Antonio, in the safety of a hotel room far from my problems, I could imagine for the first time that perhaps the weight of reconciliation was not on my shoulders alone. Maybe the "ask" that I had heard so often directed at me, and that I had posed to myself, was an inappropriate or even impossible one. Maybe the message of my body was not a problem to be overcome but actually wisdom to be embraced. Maybe my whole life, shackled to the worst memories of my past, didn't have to be collateral damage in the reconciliation that God asked of me.

David became a steadfast advocate and ally as I tried over the next months to actualize the decision I'd made. He was the person who kept his phone on when, in my effort to exit the relationship, I began to feel unsafe due to Neill's reluctance to accept my choice. David's family received mine in their home, just before Christmas, when I felt I couldn't stay any longer and needed respite. He recognized that it's one thing to tell people to leave relationships of domestic violence and another to walk alongside them to make those decisions a reality. During the difficult weeks between separation and finalization of divorce, David regularly made enough chicken noodle soup to feed the girls and me for several days at a time, quietly leaving it for me in the bottom of the work refrigerator. When I reflect back on this time, I remember that soup as one of the things that fueled my determination to persevere.

But the biggest contribution that David made to my journey was distinguishing between the reconciliation pushed on me from so many directions and God's reconciliation. God's reconciliation, David taught, wasn't the dirty word I'd come to associate with staying in a relationship where I felt unsafe. In our conversations about my desire to end the marriage, I noticed a shift in David's vocabulary. Instead of speaking about the possibility of continuing the marriage as *reconciliation*, David began to refer to it as *reunification*. Reconciliation was so much more than, and perhaps even at odds with, reunification.

I began to realize as the months wore on that I had allowed myself to settle for a false peace that involved my daily unwellness. Whenever Neill and the kids were around, I found myself suppressing, as much as I could, the painful emotions that arose in connection with the marriage, but in quiet moments by myself, they came back like a tsunami. On drives, in peaceful moments at my office, or in introspective conversations with friends, these emotions were always there.

I enviously watched friends like Penelope who could be homebodies, loving spending time in their houses on their days off, while I could not stand to be still and at home, as staying in the place where, purportedly, I belonged with my husband and kids made me feel caged. Occasionally, especially on anniversaries of traumatic events, I would leave in the car without telling Neill where I was going just to have the feeling of escape, just for the sensation of leaving the trauma behind. Often, I felt detached, watching myself perform my way through life because investing all my emotions and attention in the present meant making myself vulnerable to a person I could no longer bring myself to trust.

One day, several weeks after Neill moved out for the last time, I realized that I felt different. I woke up on a Saturday morning with no plans for the day, and I realized that I felt at home. My body felt well, not tense and hypervigilant as it had for so many years while we lived together. Traumatic memories felt integrated into my broader life story. Something within me had shifted, and maybe it was, David helped me realize, God's reconciliation. He commented, "It sounds like God is reconciling you to body, mind, and home, which are all part of the reconciliation of all things, parts that it sounds like reunification would have hindered."

In God's reconciling of all things, my body's knowledge that it had a safe place to live mattered. In God's reconciling of all things, my mind could be at peace with the unchangeable events of the past. In God's reconciling of all things, I, who had lost my sense of home over and over again to violence, would be able to rest in a safe place.

Based on the way I had often heard reconciliation talked about, the needs I had as a trauma survivor had always felt subsidiary to the bigger picture of restored relationships with those who had harmed me. My healing seemed to matter less than the wedding ring I was supposed to wear on my finger. I couldn't believe that a God who loved me would want reconciliation at the cost of my life's utter brokenness. Before David's careful reframing, I lacked the language to identify the peace I experienced at the marriage's ending as part of God's reconciliation.

Not a Reconciliation Flop

I ultimately could not nor did I desire to "heal my marriage." Reconciliation with Neill was a project too big for human hands. And God did not intervene to change my feelings or Neill's lack of accountability for the wrongs.

This does not indicate a failure of God's reconciliation. That vision for reconciliation is too small. Our thinking about reconciliation shouldn't be limited to the marital status listed on a piece of paper. God is up to something so much bigger in our lives. To use the language of 2 Samuel 14:14, we were spilled like water on the ground and could not be gathered up. Maybe a bit like David and Absalom's relationship our relationship was damaged beyond the point where it could be reconstituted the way it had been before. Maybe like Jacob and Esau's, our homeland was no longer shared territory for us.

But that didn't mean that reconciliation failed. No, reconciliation took place in each of us in our relationship with God, in our ability to work together to raise our children, and in the compassion we have for each other as individuals. The fact that this much is possible bears witness to the activity of the Spirit in our midst. It's imperfect, but it's something. Many, I know, are not so fortunate.

But as husband and wife? I came to believe that I could not be reconciled to Neill *as my husband*. For one thing, a marital relationship in which we could be reconciled no longer existed. I didn't end our relationship as husband and wife when I asked Neill to move out. I didn't end our marriage when I couldn't bring myself to wear my wedding ring any longer. I didn't end it when I signed a piece of paper. Our marriage relationship died and was buried, for me, when he physically attacked me for the first time and when he made me responsible for his life or death for the first time. Each subsequent act of aggression buried our marriage one foot deeper in the ground. Each subsequent suicidal threat engraved another letter on the tombstone. We cannot, in this life, experience reconciliation within something that is already dead. Our marriage went to a place where no one could help it.

release and rebirth

life begins, again

Releasing Our Lives?

One Sunday, right before the birth of our third daughter, the Gospel lesson during worship included these verses from John: "Very truly, I tell you, unless a grain of wheat falls into the earth and dies, it remains just a single grain, but if it dies, it bears much fruit. Those who love their life lose it, and those who hate their life in this world will keep it for eternal life" (12:24–25). Jesus, who is fast approaching his own death, urges his disciples to consider what it means to give up, to release, parts of themselves. Just as a grain of wheat loses itself to produce a field of harvest, so our release of self gives way to bountiful life.

For survivors, these verses do not feel prophetically challenging but instead heartbreakingly familiar. Some of us have heard a message to abandon our lives, to sacrifice our true identities. Some of us have heard a message to sacrifice ourselves, to lay down our lives *even to the point, at times, of our own physical, emotional, and spiritual deaths.*

Particularly for women, for people who are racial or ethnic minorities, and for survivors of abuse or other forms of violence, these words can hurt. "Be willing to give up your whole life," we hear. "Your life matters less than keeping other people, including those who hurt you, whole." This exhortation to give up our lives squares with how forgiveness is defined as well. For many theologians, the action of Jesus Christ on the cross is the crux of forgiveness. As survivors and victims of abuse, we often hear that Jesus modeled forgiveness for us, and now we have to live it out by shouldering the sins of our abusers. At least, that's what it sounds like from many books I've read.

But what about when survivors and victims have already borne the cost of abusers' sins time and time again? What about when we do not want to die, as Jesus did, for the sins of our abusers? What about when all we want is to live?

One of the contributions of Womanist theology, a field of theology centered on the lived experiences and thoughts of Black women, is an interrogation of total self-sacrifice at the expense of ourselves. Womanist theologians have explored how the idea of surrogacy, that concept of allowing our bodies and our lives to essentially be given up for others, is one that marginalized people, especially Black women in America, have faced. Delores S. Williams, a Womanist theologian, writes in her book, *Sisters in the Wilderness: The Challenge of Womanist God-Talk*:

> Jesus represents the ultimate surrogate figure; he stands in the place of someone else: sinful humankind. Surrogacy, attached to this divine personage, thus takes on an aura of the

sacred. It is therefore fitting and proper for black women to ask whether the image of a surrogate-God has salvific power for black women or whether this image supports and reinforces the exploitation that has accompanied their experience with surrogacy. If black women accept this idea of redemption, can they not also passively accept the exploitation that surrogacy brings?[1]

The challenge in Williams's words is one we all need to hear. What are we really talking about when we say that we are called to let go of ourselves, even to lose our lives, for the gospel? For those people who are already accustomed to losing their lives every day, self-sacrifice can easily be a reinforcement of the wrongful ways that society teaches us to deny ourselves the experience of the love of God.

Counting the Cost of Forgiveness

Equating interpersonal forgiveness with Jesus's action on the cross is inappropriate. Countless people are suffering in situations of abuse right now and feel they cannot leave because if they do, they will not be living up to Jesus's example of self-surrender and forgiveness. Mirroring Jesus is something we're encouraged to do, right? We can simply turn to passages like Ephesians 4:32: "Be kind to one another, tenderhearted, forgiving one another, as God in Christ has forgiven you." But while interpretations of this verse and others like it keep abused people in bondage, a contradictory message is close to my heart: "I [Jesus] came that they may have life and have it abundantly" (John 10:10).

Life has to matter. Life has to be considered. Jesus does not want us to die in the name of forgiving our abusers. And if I'm wrong, I'll happily take that up with God.

The reason I can forgive Neill is not because I am like Jesus, dying for the sins of the world. I can release Neill of his sins in relation to me *because Jesus takes care of them for both of us*. It is not up to me to provide salvation for Neill. It is not up to me to exonerate him of his sins—or condemn him for them. I can forgive Neill simply because, whatever Neill has done, it is not my responsibility to shoulder it. I release Neill to the future—one I hope is filled with blessings—that God has for him.

Jesus's forgiveness is both a model for my forgiveness and different from my forgiveness. It all hinges on Jesus's nature. Fully human, Jesus experiences, with me and with all suffering people, the pain of the world. Fully human, he prays, "Father, forgive them, for they do not know what they are doing" (Luke 23:34). But fully God, Jesus cosmically resolves sin in a way that I cannot. Fully God, he can shoulder the sins of the whole world. Fully God, he freely made the choice to die.

There may be some faint echoes of Jesus's sacrificial love in how I've chosen to relate to Neill.

- I filed for a no-fault divorce, choosing, at least in name, a way of exiting the relationship that did not punish Neill.

- Though I have full residential custody of the kids, Neill has overnight visitation twice a week, which is both a break for me and sometimes extraordinarily painful, especially on holidays.

- I support Neill's relationship with our daughters, which means that sometimes I hear them say things like "I wish Mommy and Daddy lived together" and I can't respond with a laundry list of all the reasons why we don't.

- I hold Neill's interests as highly as my own, and I choose to make my way through the world without financial assistance from him so that he has the greatest chance of thriving.

- I surrender my right to ask justified questions of Neill, questions I would really like to know the answers to, questions I will likely never resolve.

Forgiveness has a cost; its grace is not cheap for me, even though I've also experienced freedom through it. My forgiveness means that I relinquish my expectation that Neill can provide healing for what he has done—because that is healing he can never give me.

Nevertheless, I can count the cost and still recognize that ending my relationship en route to forgiving Neill was important, necessary, and ultimately freeing. The cost for me is, however, different than the cost for Christ, because I haven't taken the totality of Neill's sins in the relationship on myself in the way that Jesus paid for the sins of the world. Forgiveness is an invitation for me to live in freedom and not die in bondage.

What Can We Release?

When discussing forgiveness as release or surrender, I need to clarify some important points; otherwise, injunctions like the one in John 12, with which I opened the chapter, feel like a command to throw away our lives, especially for our abusers. That's harmful and even deadly.

First, the release God asks of us is not a surrender of our own sacred worth. The parts of our lives that we are called to release like grains that fall to the ground are not those that

161

give us dignity and worth. There are places within us that are holy and sacrosanct, and nothing we encounter in this world should ever violate them. In Jeremiah 31:33–34, God speaks through the prophet, saying, "I will put my law within them, and I will write it on their hearts; and I will be their God, and they shall be my people. No longer shall they teach one another, or say to each other, 'Know the LORD,' for they shall all know me, from the least of them to the greatest." The covenant of God, that deep, relational connection between God and us, is etched on each of our hearts. At our deepest level, we are created for life-giving relationship with God.

Our true selves, the parts of ourselves that mirror the image of God, are not what God asks us to abandon. What we must shed are the layers that do not reflect God's image. Sometimes layers of self-absorption stop us from fully loving our neighbor. Sometimes layers of self-defense, like a turtle's shell, prevent us from fully receiving love. These are the parts we can fittingly release.

Second, the surrenders we make must be our own choice, not born of fear of abuse. There are times when we can feel as if we're forced into a corner and ordered under coercion to give up everything. I think about the many times I asked Neill for a divorce but surrendered that insistence because of his threats. That's not how God's invitation to self-surrender goes. Even Jesus, on the brink of losing his own life, had a choice. He debated going down a different road. In John, Jesus's prayer comes from a deep disturbance within him: "Now my soul is troubled. And what shall I say—'Father, save me from this hour'?" (12:27). Jesus's soul was shaken in such a deep way that, translated from the Greek, it was literally quaking.

Jesus did not surrender his life because God or anyone else forced him to. Jesus acted as our Savior out of love, not because he was afraid of losing God's favor if he did not do so. God the Father is not an abuser who insisted that his Son die on the cross. Jesus's sacrifice has power and meaning because he acted in freedom. This point is crucial for anyone who has been told to surrender themselves under unjust circumstances. If the forces of darkness around us press upon us and ask us to sacrifice ourselves, we should be suspicious. If choices are demanded of us that invalidate our divine image, we can rightly say no. These are not sacrifices we are expected to make. The relinquishments that God invites us into actually challenge the oppressions that threaten true wholeness.

Release and surrender are the beginning of life and generativity. The new life we encounter through letting go draws us into the reign of God and pushes us away from the dominion of evil. John explains the generativity of release through the metaphor of grain falling to the ground. My rudimentary horticultural understanding is that once a plant starts to grow out of the seed, the shell of the seed falls away and decomposes. Jesus's death on the cross is transformational, as Jesus, through surrender, conquers the forces of evil in the world. Jesus tells his disciples, "Now the ruler of this world will be driven out" (John 12:31). This could also be rendered, "Now the ruler of this world will be exposed" (my translation). The crucifixion of Jesus not only drives out the powers of this world but also exposes them for what they are. The forces of evil that brought about Jesus's trip to the cross are those that his death banished and exposed as weaker than God's love. In letting go of his mortal life, Jesus unraveled the forces of evil.

This last point resonates most as I consider my story. On the surface, the flawed and dangerous advice that I received from other Christians could falsely mimic the self-surrender the gospel asks of us. But I am certain that this was not the desire of the good God who knows and loves me. I *did* choose a path of release, of surrender. I surrendered a life that kept me in bondage, a life ruled by sin. The life God calls us to release is the life that separates us from what is truly God's. Whatever hinders our testimony of God's goodness, beauty, strength, and freedom, that is what God calls us to release. Sometimes we have to release our fear that the forces of evil are actually stronger than God. We have to release our allegiance to them to embrace the kingdom of God. Sometimes we have to release our commitment to human relationships in which we find only interpersonal imprisonment rather than freedom under God's just reign.

Birthing Life from Trauma

Releasing a commitment to my relationship with Neill was where I landed. In a way, the end of the story of my marriage could be told very shortly and simply: Neill and I got divorced. In the end, I knew I could not move forward from the abuse, even after it had ended, as long as I stayed in our marriage. Within our marriage, what he had done was unforgivable. I signed a paper to end my pain and his.

But that wouldn't be the full story. I encountered freedom given by the God who makes all things new. And in that new life, there was forgiveness. The full story is that, through walking alongside dear friends, I experienced new life. Rebirth, even. So that's the story I'm going to share.

I'm no stranger to birth stories. At the time of this writing, I've given birth to three children. Birth hasn't always been easy for me. The birth of my second child was traumatic. On the evening of September 8, 2018, three weeks before my due date, I knew for certain, as I had for many months, that I did not want to be married. I told Neill I wanted to end the marriage. Immediately, he lunged at me and briefly grabbed me. I screamed, and he realized, I think, that he was losing control yet again. He stopped. "I'm leaving," he told me. "I'm killing myself."

After he left, I felt contractions starting. I'd felt them before. I called a friend and told her, "Neill's in crisis. He says he's going to kill himself. He left. I'm not sure whether he's going for the river or the train tracks or poisons this time. And I think I'm going into labor. What am I going to do if I'm in labor and Neill's like this?"

"You're not in labor," my friend told me. "Relax."

Thirty minutes later, Neill came back. He was calmer, but he was really out of it. He was talking in frightening ways that I'd never heard before. He seemed dissociated from reality, speaking about immanent threats in vague and impersonal terms. "They're coming for me. They're coming for me. If they come for me, I'm gonna kill them. We're all going to die."

"Neill, Neill, it's okay." I tried to calm him as I had done many times before. "I'm not sure who you're talking about, but they're not coming for you."

I would have kept going, but I felt a *pop*, and I knew my water had broken.

I whispered, "Oh, God, not right now." I met Neill's eyes. "Neill, my water just broke. I don't know what's going on with you, but I really need you to hold it together for just a little bit while I go have a baby."

Neill fell to his knees, wrapping his arms around my stomach. My breath was short and panicked. "Oh, my God. I am so sorry. Please forgive me. I'll be the perfect husband, the perfect father. Just keep me. Let me be there for the birth of my daughter. Let us have this family. Please. I'll do anything. I'm pleading with you."

In that moment, I felt nothing except the desire to have my baby in a safe way and in a safe place. "Okay," I said. "Okay. Let's just get the babysitter and go to the hospital."

That night, while Neill slept in the recliner in the corner of the hospital room, I labored. I was not alone, as a doula was with me, but I was aware that the man who had abused me and who was the father of my child was near me in the room. When my labor intensified and I entered transition, the doula woke him up. He came to support me, but his touch on my body intensified my pain. The tension I felt from his presence increased the pain of my labor. Naked in front of him, a baby coming out of my exposed body, I felt more violated than I ever had.

I gave birth anyway. I had no choice. I breathed out my baby, as she effortlessly arrived without even an attempt to push on my part. "We did it, baby girl," I whispered over and over. "We did it. *You and me.*" In spite of abuse, in spite of overwhelming pain, I let life be born through me.

The next night in the hospital, Neill became unhinged again. He screamed at me hours after I'd given birth. He left the hospital, threatening suicide.

The nurses came in and whispered questions to me, asking if I was safe. Traumatized by my previous experiences reporting his behavior, I told them that he was fine and was getting help. I wish I had simply told them, there at the hospital where presumably personnel could have protected me, that I couldn't go home with him. But I was too afraid.

And, well, my fear was justified. Within twenty-four hours of my return home from the hospital with my baby, Child Protective Services (CPS) was there, threatening to take my brand-new baby, whom I was breastfeeding when they arrived, and my confused one-year-old, who had been napping.

I had not tried hard enough to leave, CPS workers told me. I had caused the violence, they told me.

"He didn't hurt me. There's been a mistake," I told them, terrified.

Again, the home that CPS could see in front of them was safe. I did not pose any threats to the safety of my children and neither, in his calmed-down and medicated state, did Neill. CPS left again, taking no action except frightening me.

That birth—the way it started, continued, and ended—scarred me. It never should have gone the way it did. I should not have had to experience the pain of birth while still reeling from the pain of abuse. That experience was one that threatened to shatter me, that returned in my dreams, even as I relished every minute with my tiny new baby girl.

Birth can contribute to trauma. But birth can also redeem.

Fast-forward to my third pregnancy, when I was living as a single mom, unable to finalize our divorce in Indiana while expecting. My sweet friend Penelope volunteered as a birth partner. When I experienced possible premature labor, Penelope accompanied me to the hospital on multiple occasions to get me checked out. In a way, though inconvenient, those experiences in labor and delivery, where she and I ate snacks, swapped sister stories, and laughed until we almost peed our pants, began to reclaim the experience of labor and birth for me.

But the day of my third daughter's birth completed the ultimate repair, though I don't think Penelope was even aware of the change happening. Earlier that day, Penelope and I took our kids to a trampoline park, and I literally jumped for joy, knowing that my pregnancy was almost over and that I'd made it to the thirty-seven-week mark: strong, single, and safe. Later that afternoon, contractions started in earnest, and I encouraged them to continue by taking a two-mile walk with one foot on the sidewalk and one on the street, an old laboring mother's trick.

At about 5 p.m., I called Penelope to tell her I was in labor. I drove over to her house with all my labor gear in tow. I bounced on my birth ball in the kitchen and labored pleasantly while chatting with Lucas and Penelope as they did dishes and plied me with a small bowl of Greek yogurt and berries.

"Mom, can you *please* just take Miss Susannah to the hospital?" their ten-year-old son asked nervously.

I was happy and comfortable laboring there, but due to the increasing worries of my friends that I'd end up delivering my baby in their bathroom, Penelope and I drove to the hospital.

"Let's make a bet on when she's gonna be born!" Penelope said enthusiastically as she carried my bag through the ER entrance.

"She wants to labor in the birthing tub," Penelope instructed my nurses. They promptly and accidentally flooded my birthing suite with water, but by then I was past caring. My pain had increased to a level I found difficult to endure.

"Susannah," Penelope whispered, stroking my hair away from my face as I sat on a birth ball, "you are so beautiful, wise, and strong. I know you can do this."

"I can't do this," I protested. "I want an epidural, now, please. This is a really bad idea. Let's do this another day."

"Did you hear the woman?" Penelope called out. "She said she wants an epidural, *now!*"

But then I felt overwhelming pressure. "Listen to your body," my midwife whispered. "You can do what it's telling you."

I pushed slightly, and my water broke. I stood up to allow the nurses to clean up the puddle of fluid, and, I lie not, my baby began to slide out.

"She's coming!" I cried, not in the slightest pain but in joy. In power and strength, my body birthed the baby I'd longed to hold. The midwife, who had no idea I was about to deliver, didn't even have her gloves on. Penelope and I stood across the bed from each other, holding hands and laughing. "Susannah, you just birthed a baby!" Penelope told me. I couldn't believe it was over. The midwife passed my baby through my legs to me as I stood in triumph, realizing that I had done it.

The whole birth was an incredible, positive experience. There was nothing to fear. The shadows of the past slipped far into the background as I experienced the accompaniment of a circle of strong women. My youngest daughter was born into laughter and love.

From this birth, I learned a powerful lesson: Sometimes we do face situations that feel too much to handle, when we wish we could take all the pain away. Yet sometimes we stand and deliver. Sometimes we rise strong and triumphant from the pain. Sometimes hope is born.

Penelope's presence at my third delivery changed my relationship with the trauma of the second. Her love and support, which she offered so freely as my birth partner, meant that the third time I was in labor I felt safe, loved, and chosen. The most important memory I now have of birth is not a labor begun with threats and abuse but a time when my friend accompanied me while I fearlessly delivered my child.

In the face of such love and safety, even the power of trauma starts to lose its sway. Birth doesn't erase the past, but birth can redeem pain and turn it into a story that ends with beauty.

Forgiveness and Rebirth

Rebirth is at the heart of what forgiveness is for me now. The image of birth, and how it transforms everything, is subtly different from the language of release that's become popular in therapeutic circles. Contemporary mental health professionals often emphasize release of painful emotions like anger as part of the healing process.[2] I have found help and truth in this model. However, I don't think the word *release* fully encompasses what I experienced along my journey.

When I hear "release," I hear "letting go." Yet pain like I've known, like so many people have known, doesn't just get let go or set down. The pain I have known has become a part of me—and I wouldn't want even forgiveness to take away the wisdom and grace I have gained from my experiences. I didn't dump my trauma somewhere like off-loaded cargo. The love I experienced from God and my friends transformed the experience of that pain from something that almost destroyed me into something that rebirthed me. I'm not saying the abuse was a blessing. But through God working despite my experiences, I have been made new. And that making new—rebirth—is at the essence of what forgiveness has become for me.

The idea of birth as transformation is at least as old as Scripture itself. One of the many ways that Scripture describes God is as a laboring mother who travails in her labor to bring forth a new world. Isaiah portrays God as a laboring mother in this way:

> For a long time I have held my peace,
>   I have kept still and restrained myself;
> now I will cry out like a woman in labor;
>   I will gasp and pant. (42:14)

When God is working out something new, working toward the renewal of the world, God is having contractions.

Humans mirror God in going into metaphorical labor when they're experiencing transformative forgiveness. It's painful, prolonged, and sometimes utterly amazing. Accordingly, Isaiah also writes about how God's people, portrayed as a woman, labor and deliver as they are on the cusp of change.

> Before she was in labor
>   she gave birth;
> before her pain came upon her
>   she delivered a son.
> Who has heard of such a thing?
>   Who has seen such things?
> Shall a land be born in one day?
>   Shall a nation be delivered in one moment?
> Yet as soon as Zion was in labor
>   she delivered her children.
> Shall I open the womb and not deliver?
>   says the Lord;
> shall I, the one who delivers, shut the womb?
>   says your God. (66:7–9)

God facilitates the birthing process and delivery as the good midwife who takes care of the laboring mother through the entire experience. (I've had a few of those midwives!) God invites these experiences of transformation, of "opening the womb." God is also faithfully with us as we experience the birth pangs of transformation, as we push and breathe to bring new life into the world. We need not fear that we travail in vain.

The metaphor of labor and delivery as ushering in God's new world is found in the New Testament as well. In Romans, the suffering of the world is like a laboring mother's pains: "We know that the whole creation has been groaning together as it suffers together the pains of labor, and not only the creation, but we ourselves, who have the first fruits of the Spirit, groan inwardly while we wait for adoption, the redemption of our bodies" (8:22–23). Not just humans but *all of creation* is groaning in labor pains. We long for birth to come to transform these pains from suffering into new life. Even in the pain, there is potential for life.

In the life and teachings of Jesus, birth plays a significant role. Most famous, of course, is Jesus's weird gynecological discussion with Nicodemus, who is desperate to know how he can see the kingdom of God.

> Jesus answered him, "Very truly, I tell you, no one can see the kingdom of God without being born from above." Nicodemus said to him, "How can anyone be born after having grown old? Can one enter a second time into the mother's womb and be born?" Jesus answered, "Very truly, I tell you, no one can enter the kingdom of God without being born of water and Spirit. What is born of the flesh is flesh, and what is born of the Spirit is spirit. Do not be astonished that I said to you, 'You must be born from above.'" (John 3:3–7)

When Jesus wants to talk about life-altering change, through which ordinary people enter the kingdom of God, the imagery of birth works for him. Especially given the patriarchal society that John is from and writing in, this is stunning. Experiencing the type of transformation that brings a person into God's presence is like being birthed once again—not by entering a mother's womb but through the mothering role of the Spirit.

The theme of birth continues in John even through Jesus's death on the cross. John understands Jesus's death on the cross in terms of a laboring mother. Perhaps shockingly for many of us who are used to thinking about Jesus's masculinity, Jesus's wounds are much like those of a birthing mother: "One of the soldiers pierced his side with a spear, and at once blood and water came out" (John 19:34). Blood and water. Water and blood. There isn't a "clean" way to push a baby out. Waters break, sometimes suddenly and abruptly, as mine did with my middle daughter, signaling a moment of crisis. Sometimes they break to herald the joyful arrival of new life. But there's water. And there's blood. As a first-time mother, I naively didn't realize how much I'd bleed after I gave birth. And it continued for about six weeks.

So when Jesus on the cross leaks blood and water, the leaky mamas of this world like me can relate to his experience. Jesus births God's people into transformation when he dies on the cross and is raised from the grave. He births us from darkness into life, from hunger into fullness, from loneliness into family, from hate into love. He births us from death into life. The one whom Mary pushed out of her womb births new humanity from himself. Life wins, again.

That's where I find the hope of forgiveness in Jesus's passion: not that, like Jesus, I can reasonably carry the sins of the whole world, or even the sins of my abuser, but that God births life again despite the presence of the specter of death. In light of that new life, everything feels different. Everything *is* different. The violence of oppression is no longer supreme. And because of that, I can forgive.

So when I think about my forgiveness journey, I frame it in terms of birth. Forgiveness means rebirthing one's experience of the world so that the wrongs that caused the valid feelings of hurt and anger need no longer be at the center. Simple "release" is not safe if the circumstances that caused the hurt remain the same. Often the hurt and anger must remain in the center while abuse or its aftermath is still close by. In my case, removing the marriage to rebirth the terms of the relationship with my husband made forgiveness possible.

Joseph's Forgiveness

As I sought to understand the rebirth I experienced through forgiveness, I looked to the complexity of human relationships in Scripture. In this search, I found Joseph, who extends a costly grace to his brothers.

Joseph's status as a privileged child earns him his brothers' hatred. So Joseph's brothers sell him into slavery and deliver the news to his father, Jacob, that Joseph is dead, torn apart by wild animals. Joseph ends up in Egypt, which seems okay at first, until he gets thrown in prison because his master's wife abuses him and then flips the script so she's the victim and he's the abuser. Jacob's dream interpretation ability gets him out of prison and into Pharaoh's confidences, until he's second only to Pharaoh in Egypt.

Joseph seems to have done well for himself. The effects of the horrible wrong done to him are mitigated. But Joseph has not yet reckoned with his brothers, who have had absolutely nothing to do with the good things that have happened to him. Then a famine strikes and Egypt is set up for success through Joseph's wise preparations. Joseph's family is in trouble, and so Joseph's brothers, having no idea that their brother is now in Egypt, make the trek down to buy food.

When Joseph is reunited with his brothers, an emotional rebirth takes place in a moment of forgiveness. Joseph does not seek to make his former abusers bear the wrong he experienced but instead blesses them. Joseph promises to provide for his family, to support them tangibly, despite what they did. Joseph helps to arrange the settlement in Goshen of his father and his brothers so that everyone is in Egypt together. And that is where they'll be until the beginning of the next book of the Bible, Exodus, when a new king reigns who did not know Joseph. Of course, this cozy family setup isn't the norm in cases of abuse.

Contrary to what some Christians have said about forgiveness, forgiveness is oftentimes not simply about the person who forgives. There also can be a benefit to the person who is forgiven. The offender may be released from the debt they owe—because with the kind of offenses we are talking about, repayment would be impossible—even while they are also held accountable.

In the Joseph story, there is a material element to the forgiveness Joseph extends. He does not keep any of his brothers in prison. He gives them grain. Technically, he owes them none of this. If he were dead or enslaved in a foreign land, the way the brothers intended him to be, he would not be available to make these provisions. Nothing entitles the brothers to the resources and mercy that Joseph offers. Ultimately, Joseph's family, including his brothers, settles in Egypt. So the brothers profit from Joseph's forgiveness. This is the "objective" or "forensic" forgiveness, in which someone's debts are canceled, that traditionally has dominated Christian understandings. Joseph's forgiveness *does something* for his brothers.

Yet Joseph in no way "absorbs" the offenses of his brothers. He is no longer living in slavery. He is no longer in prison or exploited by his superiors. If he were still being exploited, then his response to his brothers might be quite different. Now that he is not suffering the consequences of his abusers' actions, at least not in the same way as he was in the pit or in overt slavery, he is free to respond to his brothers authentically and openly.

God moves Joseph from a place of bondage to a place of freedom. Experiencing what God can do *in spite of* the worst of human behavior moves Joseph to forgiveness. God has not ceased to act and in fact has done much more with Joseph's life than Joseph could have ever imagined, and this realization brings Joseph to this place. Joseph's forgiveness does *not* include absorption of the sins of his brothers. The family's conversation shows this nuance:

> Realizing that their father was dead, Joseph's brothers said, "What if Joseph still bears a grudge against us and pays us back in full for all the wrong that we did to him?" So they approached Joseph, saying, "Your father gave this instruction before he died, 'Say to Joseph: "I beg you, forgive the crime of your brothers and the wrong they did in harming you."' Now therefore please forgive the crime of the servants of the God of your father." Joseph wept when they spoke to him. Then his brothers also wept, fell down before him, and said, "We are here as your slaves." But Joseph said to them, "Do not be afraid! Am I in the place of God? Even though you intended to do harm to me, God intended it for good, in order to preserve a numerous people, as he is doing today. So do not fear; I myself will provide for you and your little ones." In this way he reassured them, speaking kindly to them. (Gen. 50:15–21)

Joseph's response to his brothers ties together release of self *and* release of others. For Joseph, as I experienced in my own story, tears are a sign of emotional rebirth. The biblical story leaves undefined the reason that Joseph weeps. It could be because his brothers have finally owned up to their behavior. It could be the realization that *he* is now in a position to help the people who once harmed him. It could be that he is finally experiencing the full range of emotion that he had suppressed to survive his kidnapping, enslavement, and imprisonment. Whatever the reason, as Joseph prepares to speak words of grace to his brothers and hears their words to him, he weeps. He relinquishes his right to vengeance in light of what God has done in bringing good even through the terrors of his experience.

Joseph's story shows that neither forgiveness as therapeutic release nor forgiveness as mercy toward an offender needs to stand alone. Grace is not cheapened when a person who forgives experiences catharsis. Nor does the fact that forgiveness creates benefits for the offending person mitigate the renewal for the forgiver. Joseph sheds tears at this moment when both come together. The only way I have found to hold together these realities and acknowledge the goodness of God in the midst of them is through tears. I have found no words to adequately express the intensity of emotion that culminates when everyone goes free. Tears are the birth waters of forgiveness as the trauma of the past metamorphoses into fragile new life.

Tears of Freedom

One of the most important lessons I learned on my forgiveness journey is that choosing to end my marriage didn't mean that the love had to end. I chose to honor and surrender my love by placing it squarely at God's feet instead of carrying it and consummating it in its fullest expressions. I didn't have to stop loving Neill, even as the ways that my love takes shape have inevitably changed over time.

I began to experience this unburdening one evening at Lucas and Penelope's house. On that occasion, I realized that I'd come to the point of needing to both acknowledge and release my love for Neill.

After Lucas and Penelope prayed for me that night, the weight of their hands pressing the warmth of God's love onto my shoulders, I prayed too. I prayed for my love to no longer be a burden that controlled me and dictated my choices but instead to be a beautiful gift that we'd shared. I prayed for it to become a gift that I could pass on to God. I prayed that my love, though limited and temporal in my marriage, would be a whole and fitting offering to God, held forever in God's timeless hands. I prayed for only the best of my love to continue to follow Neill as he walked, free, down his own path.

As happened often when my friends and I prayed together on this journey, by the end of this prayer, my tears were splashing into my outstretched hands. This time, though, I could see that Lucas and Penelope were crying as well.

"The waterworks," Lucas remarked, wiping his eyes.

There were no words to match the experience of knowing that my love toward Neill was too big to hold him in bondage to the past. No words, but tears sufficed.

Self-Forgiveness

This journey of rebirth has been an ongoing one, and it has expanded in directions I did not expect. Forgiving Neill was not nearly as hard as I would have thought it would be. When the immediacy of the trauma lifted, because Neill had moved out during one of our separations, I could easily feel a grace for Neill sweeping in like the tide. The burdens of what he had done to me felt lighter quickly; absence seemed to make my heart more forgetful of its pain.

It was because of this, in part, that my marriage continued on paper as long as it did. If Neill left for a time, the sense of relief would be so great—even in the midst of the grief of losing my closest friend, partner, and co-parent—that I would believe that something permanent had shifted within me. The trauma seemed behind me enough for our marriage to feel whole and safe to me. Then I would invite Neill to come home. But again I would feel the brokenness that made forgiveness feel false and fleeting, and I would feel myself falling out of forgiveness as if tumbling awake from a dream. I could not offer it to him while he was present in my home. The deepest parts of me would not allow it. I'd again see him filtered through the worst moments of our lives.

Extending a more substantial forgiveness to Neill was, in the end, a matter of letting the safety of my mind, body, and spirit be as important as his for once. It was only in these conditions when I no longer gave away my life in the name of caring for Neill that I knew, most deeply, that I could really forgive Neill. And yet extending that same forgiveness to myself during our last pre-divorce separation felt much more difficult.

Even when we know, *we know*, that what happened to us wasn't our fault, sometimes it's hard to release ourselves from the shame of the choices we made in the process. As much as forgiveness of Neill was part of my story, forgiving myself was its own process. And forgiving myself was the hardest part of all.

Rebirth was about letting Neill go—and also about letting go of the heavy burden of guilt I felt for ending the relationship. Because Neill had placed the weight of his life in my hands, it was challenging to end the relationship without feeling as if I'd ruined his life. This guilt tied me to Neill longer than anything else. As spouses and as parents of our children, our emotional ties ran deep. Severing any of those bonds was painful, mainly because I wanted him to know how deeply I loved him in spite of everything.

In the absence of the ongoing reminder of trauma (Neill himself) and in the absence of the ongoing fear, anger, and pain brought by his presence, I found it difficult to justify, even to myself, the choice I had made to end the relationship. Neill worked alongside me as an attentive father to our girls and a co-parent. Our interactions, though typically brief and intentionally limited to communicating about the girls' needs, were usually warm and pleasant. Even after the papers were signed and the marriage was really and truly over, I found myself tormented with misgivings: *What have I done? Have I ruined the lives of everyone in my family? Have I destroyed any future we could have had?*

"This is the best-case scenario," David reminded me. "Remember that Neill is calm and stable now in part because this pressure cooker of a situation is turned off. One of my hopes for your relationship with him moving forward has been that one day he'll be such a good father and co-parent and you'll feel so safe around him that you'll wonder why you had to do this. And I know that will be difficult to process at times. But I'm also here to remind you that you did have to do this, and if you'd like, I can recall for you the unsafe moments when you knew that most clearly."

As the immediacy of the trauma faded, it was not only ending the relationship but also what I had done in the course of experiencing abuse and trying to leave that weighed heavily on me. The choices I had made during intense moments of life and death became harder for me to contend with as I felt more removed from their shadows. I processed how I had called 911, bringing police who handcuffed and hospitalized Neill under poor conditions. I was still haunted by the idea that Neill, a Black man with mental illness, could become a person whose name was chanted in protest of police brutality. I didn't know how to hold in tension both my vulnerability as a young mother and my privilege as a White woman.

My guilt was complicated. Not only did I viscerally despise my role in bringing Neill into contact with state systems, but I also despised the fact that it took me so long to keep my promise to myself that I'd never stay in a relationship with someone who hurt me. I hated that I had held out hope for so long and had welcomed him back again and again in spite of my gut knowledge that our relationship would never work. I had not taken the most self-protective steps I could; I had lied for him and protected him; I had been afraid of his retaliation; I had seemed to care more about my career trajectory and financial stability than my physical and emotional safety; I had been unable to bear the thought of removing our children from his daily presence. And in the process, I felt as though I had given away the past five years of my life in the blink of an eye for a relationship that was never going to honor my God-given needs.

There was another part of myself that saw the real work and growth in Neill, evidence that he was moving in a positive direction, and I wondered if initiating the divorce was a failure to give him enough credit. But I knew by then that no matter what Neill did, I could not desire the marriage anymore.

I told Lucas and Penelope about these complicated emotions at one of our meetings. "I feel so guilty," I confessed to them.

Lucas shook his head, seemingly confused. "What could you feel guilty for, Susannah?" he asked.

I answered, "Looking back on everything, I see so many things I could have done differently that would have relieved pain for both Neill and me. Now I'm on the precipice of

ending the relationship, and looking at who Neill is now, I
wonder whether God will understand."

"Well, you know God," Lucas replied. "He loves you as
a daughter, fiercely and protectively, more than we can even
understand. So you tell us, Susannah, what do you think God
would say to you if you brought this guilt to him?"

"I think he would say, 'Go and live,'" I said, uncertain. "I
think he would understand. But it's difficult for me to feel
that acceptance. It's difficult for me to emotionally know
that, although I do intellectually."

"We'll keep knowing that for you until you can know it
emotionally," Lucas said. "And we pray that the day comes
when you do feel God's acceptance, fully."

As I waited for my divorce to be finalized, I wanted to
know, ultimately, how God could accept *me*, the person who
had been tasked with impossible decisions and had taken the
marriage to the chopping block. The collective weight of all
my paradoxical guilt—for staying too long, for leaving too
soon, for Neill's endangerment, for my endangerment—was
more than the burden of anger and pain I carried for Neill's
actions. As the time of our separation lengthened and the
time for signing the divorce papers drew near, I felt no blame
or rage toward Neill. It seemed as though the forgiveness
mission might have been successful. What I carried toward
myself was the real burden—a burden that made the prospect
of signing the final papers a lot more complicated. Could I
really unburden us all so easily?

The months leading up to signing the divorce papers felt
interminable. On the one hand, I longed to sign and for
the marriage to be over. During delays in the legal process,
I felt inexorably stuck, as if having already withdrawn my
consent to the marriage, I was still being forced to remain
within it. In other words, the delay felt like an assault. On

the other hand, part of me doubted that I could walk this road to its conclusion. How could I sign a paper separating my life, in legal ways at least, from the life that had cleaved to mine for so long?

After months of waiting, I finally got the call that the papers were ready and I needed to visit my attorney's office on Monday to sign. When I received this news, my body began to shake uncontrollably. I knew that it was in my power to end the stagnant pain of this story, but I wasn't sure if I could find the strength to do it. Even after all the conversations with Lucas and Penelope and David, I felt as though this was a final exam I might actually flunk. The finality of divorce seemed like it could be, after all, a failure at forgiveness.

And yet I knew, *I knew*, this had to be done. There was no other way for me to live a life undefined by its worst moments. There was no way for me to share my body, mind, and soul with Neill as one flesh without feeling like my safety and dignity were compromised. I knew I wanted to sign, but I wasn't sure how I'd ever accomplish it.

I told David the papers were ready and that I needed to go to the office to finish the process. "Okay," David responded calmly. "Do you want me to accompany you?"

"Yes, please," I responded. "And don't let me bail."

"I won't," David promised. "Even if I have to remind you of what you've said today."

With twenty-four hours left before signing, I felt as though I was going to die, not because I thought my choice was wrong but because the words Neill had spoken to me several years before—that he would kill me if I tried to divorce him—were ringing in my ears. These had not been idle threats. They had been accompanied by physical violence that had actually endangered me. Despite the degrees of healing that had taken place in intervening years, in the hours before the signing, that physical violence felt like not a memory but a present reality. Signing felt like assenting to my death sentence. I expected Neill to come and make good on his promise.

All this was taking place during Holy Week. The day before the signing, I preached a sermon at David's church about Jesus's agony on the Mount of Olives, when his disciples numbed themselves into sleep and only an angel's presence strengthened him. "Take this cup from me," Jesus prays, bloody tears falling. Those last hours were my own vigil as I waited to drink from a cup I didn't order as a twenty-four-year-old bride. In the intensity of those hours, I felt like that cup would kill me too.

David named the parallel between my Holy Week sermon and the moment of confronting my trauma through signing. "I will not fall asleep in your time of agony. We'll do this together," he promised me.

And that's what happened. I don't think I would have gone to my lawyer's office if he hadn't driven me there. I don't think I would have gone into the office if he hadn't gotten out of the car first. And I don't think I would have signed if he hadn't quietly represented the belief that there was hope for me beyond my marriage. Even as I sat in my attorney's office, the papers to end my marriage spread in front of me, thoughts raced through my mind: *What if I hadn't tried hard enough? What if Neill's seeming acceptance of the divorce meant that his behavior had changed enough that my decision was no longer justified? What if he exploded after he found out that I signed, and I died—or he did? What if?*

I met David's eyes. "What if I die after I sign?"

"You won't," he told me.

"I don't know that."

"Susannah. You told me not to let you bail."

I looked down at the papers. The line on the decree of dissolution was waiting for my signature. I had known for five years that I would one day need to sign on that line, but the few strokes of the pen that were needed to end it all felt beyond me.

David spoke again. My mind was whirling so fast that I didn't catch most of it. All I heard of what he said was "life." I'm sure he said things more profound than that, but the one word was all I needed. Life was what God spoke into being at creation. Life was what Christ came to bring: "In him was life . . ." (John 1:4). Life was the keystone of what I'd "heard" months earlier at the Alamo, the invitation to leave, survive, and *live*.

Life was what I wanted. To have the life that God wanted for me. To share that life, the life of God within me, with my girls, with my community, and with God's world. Maybe even to have a chance at life with a partner, unknown to me then, who would not hurt me.

Slowly, painfully, I signed the last page.

"I need to get out of here," I stated flatly.

I didn't cry until we were well away from the office. And when I did cry, it was five years' worth of tears. But of one thing I was certain: I was not weeping for the actual relationship I was ending. I was crying for the relationship I thought I would have when I got married seven years earlier. For the lost innocence of the young woman who had promised her life to a young man who was good, kind, and safe. For the lost innocence of the young man who had made decisions he never planned to but that did deep harm, who has struggled with self-hatred ever since. For a future of mutual trust, of growing old together, that I would never share with him. For the home of safety and support I could never create with him for our girls and ourselves. For the past of pain, undeserved, that malformed Neill's emotional responses in ways that were dangerous and aggressive. For five years of my life in which I reexperienced traumatic moments daily while living with him.

I grieved all this as we drove away from the attorney's office, and yet the ending of the marriage, in the form it had taken, was not among my griefs that day. I knew there was no other way.

Even as my tears fell, my nose ran, my body rocked back and forth seeking comfort—and I wondered if David, not only a friend and pastor but also a colleague, would ever respect me again after seeing me completely lose it—I realized that I was feeling something I had not felt fully before.

It was forgiveness.

In signing the papers, in finalizing the divorce, I believe that I found forgiveness, safe and sound, in the still, small voice of God. Forgiveness was not, and never had been, found in staying in emotional or physical unsafety. It didn't mean giving away my life in the futile pursuit of Neill's permanent happiness. Forgiveness meant rebirth, for both Neill and me. By signing the papers, I released him from the burden of responsibility for the past, a burden that he seemed unable and unwilling to accept. He couldn't pay back what he owed me, ever, and I released him from the responsibility of trying (or the guilt of failing to try). I rebirthed myself from the pain of the past, which had inevitably stalked me while I lived with my now ex-husband.

The permanent end of our marriage meant that it was safe for my body to stop carrying the burden of pain as intensely. The immediacy of the trauma could fade. I could release myself from the guilt of failing at the impossible task of going back to the way things were. I could extend to myself the grace of listening to what my body and emotions had told me for many years, whispering to them, "You are good. You are safe now." In doing all this, I stepped more fully into the knowledge that both Neill and I are God's beloved children.

Divorce didn't represent the failure of forgiveness. Instead, divorce represented, in my story anyway, the extension of the greatest forgiveness possible under the circumstances the abuse had handed me. I wept in the car because I knew I hadn't failed. The tears signaled the beginning of wholeness.

Rebirthing parts of ourselves, releasing parts of our old lives, is hard. The book of Hebrews states that Jesus made this release of his own life into God's hands with "loud cries and tears, to the one who was able to save him from death" (5:7). If Jesus cried over releasing his life, then I'm sure we can do the same. Even when release leads us out of the dominion of evil and deeper into the grace and love of God, it is painful to let go of what we know.

Poised as we were within Holy Week, I felt the tension of the cross and the empty tomb. For years and yet also particularly dramatically on that Monday, I had experienced the torturous death of our relationship and the forsakenness of living daily with traumatic memories. I had felt the death of losing myself and the one I loved to domestic violence. And yet I knew, as I sat with tears flowing in the car, that the words resounding in my mind, "It is finished," would usher in new hope. The tomb was empty for me that day too. The grave didn't win. There was life beyond the death of relationship-ending abuse, a life that had passed through hell and reigned victorious over the torment of the cross. I would live. Neill would live. Our girls would live. There would be a life in which one day this pain would be a memory and not a searing, open wound. God was making all things new.

"It's a new day," I told David.

In the pain, in the struggle, we have this hope. We have the hope that a small grain of wheat, falling to the earth and dying, can bear much fruit. We release what we know and cling to, what holds our allegiance to brokenness, in the hope that life can come from these small deaths. The rich, deep soil of Scripture nourishes our seed with the promise that God is not done with us yet. As God's tears intermingle with ours and water the soil, we'll see green shoots springing up. As the light of the Son gives life to those tiny shoots, we'll see a new garden grow. We'll remember that even in the death and falling away of winter, there's beauty. Spring is here again.

conclusion

For Victims and Survivors

If you've read this far, then you know my story. While I realized that sharing this story publicly would be intimidating, I had to tell it, because I wish someone had told me a story like mine.

I tell my story not to incriminate anyone involved, especially not Neill. But if I can be part of one other person's journey to freedom from death-dealing theologies of forgiveness and reconciliation, then my work will be worth it. I tell my story because if you are where I was, you need to know that you matter infinitely to God.

I was stuck because what I wanted for myself was at odds with what I thought a good Christian would do. Maybe you're standing at a crossroads, as I was a few years ago, not knowing how to move forward. Maybe you know what you need to do but you don't know how to do it and stay a Christian. Maybe you're scared that if you end the relationship or leave the abuse, your community will reject you. Maybe you've been waiting for a word that will let you know what you can do.

I get it. I really, truly, fundamentally get it. I stayed in a relationship five years longer than I meant to in large part because of my guilt about "failing" as a Christian by doing what I wanted to do instead of what I thought was the Christian thing to do. I don't wish away the time that gave me my three strong, beautiful, and kind daughters, but I wish I had known the freedom I have much earlier.

I wish you that freedom.

So if you're staying, as I did, because of the guilt that leaving means you failed at forgiveness, I hope you can take this from my journey: Maybe leaving doesn't mean you failed to forgive. Maybe leaving means you are so committed to forgiveness that you are willing to do whatever it takes to get there.

Even raging against the wrong that was done to you.

Even lamenting that things will never be the way you planned they'd be.

Even seeking accountability.

Even realizing that reconciliation in this life may not be possible.

Even walking away from a relationship that hurt you.

Even divorcing a person you loved.

Even being born again into a life that's whole and safe.

For Those Who Walk Alongside Survivors

I tell my story for those who walk alongside survivors too, because so much of this story is not just about me. It's about what people around me said, did, and thought. There are great moments of support that I can't talk about without getting emotional, and cringeworthy moments that probably make people (me included) want to turn tail and run from the church forever.

You're looking to do God's work of binding up the brokenhearted and providing release to the captives (Isa. 61:1).

You want to know what to say and do to represent the gospel, to bring healing in families, and to support people in scary situations that may be outside what you've seen and dealt with before. It's a lot to carry, and you need and deserve your own support too.

Here's what I can offer you, in a nutshell, from my experience:

- Presence is more important than anything you have to say.
- You won't fully understand what someone else is going through, especially if you aren't in their situation of vulnerability.
- Remember that your words and actions may carry far more weight than you realize.
- Saying that somebody should forgive or reconcile doesn't help them do it—and I don't know what a forced forgiveness or reconciliation would even mean.
- Consider whether your theology deals life or death. Consider whether you would like to see your congregant/mentee/colleague/friend dead or alive. If you had a choice, would you rather they have what you consider the wrong theology and live or have the right theology and die?
- Your perfection isn't called for. Nobody who walked alongside me had everything I needed.

My story shows that journeys of forgiveness should not be walked alone, placed as burdens on survivors. Penelope, Lucas, and David walked alongside me during my journey in life-changing ways. I love and am grateful for each of them. I hope that everyone who walks a forgiveness path finds companions as steadfast as these.

Survivors need a Penelope who listens intently and, when she speaks, fiercely demands the wellness that you've never quite dared to claim but always wanted for yourself. Survivors need a Penelope who speaks the truth to them and keeps believing that accountability is not too much to ask for. Survivors need a Penelope who will remain with them through the messy and vulnerable times of their lives, analogous to labor, to see the birth of new life.

Survivors need a Lucas who isn't afraid to ask the questions that go into hard emotional places, who has the right words at the right moment. Survivors need a Lucas who keeps articulating the beauty of God's vision in a world that's so often broken. Survivors need a Lucas who prays the bold prayers that may or may not find their resolution in seeming answers.

Survivors need a David who states as many times as necessary, "I believe you." Survivors need a David who calmly and quietly offers to accompany them to do the hard things that lead to life and freedom. Survivors need a David who recognizes that the journey continues beyond the point of immediate crisis and that practical support in the day-to-day is necessary for survivors to keep making the next hard, right choices.

Without these friends, each of them, I would still feel myself torn apart, day by day, as I tried to make a future out of a past that, for me, was irrevocably broken. Thanks to the movement of the Spirit in their ministry with me, I'm now building a future, one small LEGO brick at a time, from the choice to trust Neill to God's hands and the choice to base my own life on the hope that God is making all things new. The old has passed away; the new has come (2 Cor. 5:17).

If you're in a place where you are walking alongside someone with a story like mine, I thank you profoundly. Isolation is the friend of abuse. It's quite possible that you are part of a story in which someone's life continues in wholeness instead of ending in violence or despair. What you are doing isn't easy. Since ending my marriage, I've had the honor of walking alongside others in my roles as friend, pastor, and advocate, and I know the fear for those I have come to care for along with the feeling of a total lack of control over what happens next. Be mindful of your own wellness and that hearing about the experiences of a trauma survivor can become traumatic for you as well. There's a delicate balance between walking alongside another person in their journey and allowing another person's journey to become your own.

The Last Word: Life

I want to remind you, however you came to read this story, that there is great hope beyond abuse and trauma. There's not an erasure, nor would we want to erase all that trauma has brought us, but there can be integration of traumatic stories into a life story that has far, far more than trauma in it. With safety and work and love and the passage of time, forgiveness can sometimes manifest itself even when we revisit the old places of wounding.

I experienced this myself as I journeyed back.

About six months after my divorce was finalized, I did something I had been intending to do for a long time: I returned "home," back to Nashville, to revisit the main site of my trauma. It was the lower-middle-income apartment complex where Neill and I had lived for the most difficult period of our marriage.

I didn't go alone. I went with Michael, who had become a dear friend, confidant, and partner during the intervening period. We were on a completely unrelated road trip, but when the Batman building of Nashville flashed into view, I knew I needed to go.

"I need to go back to the apartment," I told Michael. Watching him driving my uncool minivan, I could see his tension heighten in the way he held the steering wheel.

"Are you sure?" he asked me. "Are you sure that won't put you into fight or flight?"

I laughed. "Well, I guess we can't really be sure until we go there," I told him. "But I think I'm okay. I need to go back."

Michael nodded, and we adjusted our navigation setting to bring us to the apartment.

It was a beautiful fall day in Nashville, just after Thanksgiving. It took me a little longer than I thought it would to figure out where the apartment was. There were a few entrances to the apartment complex, and we turned around a couple of times before I knew we had found it.

"Up there," I told him, pointing to the end of the row, by the gazebo, by the river.

"Okay, so are we just driving by?" Michael asked, still nervous.

"No, I need to get out," I told him, grabbing my phone as I hopped out of the minivan.

I walked up to the gazebo, sat down, and took a really hard, long look around.

It was where I had seen my ex-husband handcuffed.

It was where I had been unable to sleep.

It was where Neill had taken off his belt and threatened to hang himself with me as his audience.

It was where Child Protective Services had come.

It was where I had seen all that mattered to me in life nearly slip away from me.

I felt Michael watching me from the car, worried that all this would be too much. He might have been right that it was risky. I felt the weight of the past as I sat there that crisp fall day, but I also felt something else: freedom.

I no longer answered to the commitments of the marriage that had almost killed me. I no longer despised myself for staying in a marriage that had harmed me. I no longer resented Neill for keeping me there. I could stand in the place where Neill almost took my life and feel love for him because I no longer had to experience the imprisonment of our marriage.

I've forgiven him—for the pain he caused me, for the breaking of my dreams, and for the path I had to walk.

I've forgiven myself—for the choices I made along the way, for taking so long to leave, and for not having it within me to make the relationship survive.

If you're reading this book without a lot of hope for the world you see around you, whether your story is that of a survivor, a loved one of a survivor, or an advocate, my heart is with you. Seasons change. Stories can take turns into realms of greater light and love. We live in a world where there is not only pain, abuse, and anger but also love, connection, and maybe even forgiveness. Forgiveness isn't the magic pill that replaces the pain, abuse, and anger with healing and connection. To me, forgiveness is actually more of a symptom of recovery than part of the cure. When the pain, abuse, and anger have been addressed through safety and justice, when healing and love are present, that's when we might find forgiveness.

Maybe you wonder, as I did and still do sometimes, if you've forgiven already or if you're still on that road. While there are probably online quizzes you can use to self-evaluate your forgiveness, I prefer these words from Lucas, which he offered to me near the end of our boot camp: "I think forgiveness is not really a destination but rather a trail we walk on every day. I don't think it's really for me to say, but between you and God, where you are on that journey. But in the ways that I see you treating Neill, the affection and care with which you still speak of him, the ways you try to seek out good for him, and the spirit which you hold toward him, I can only believe that you're on the trail."

David's response to a question that I posed to him was this: "I think you have released Neill, acknowledging that he may grow and change and desiring shalom [God's peace] in his life, while at the same time taking steps toward your shalom, recognizing that those steps may not be down the same path."

My journey with forgiveness is ongoing. I welcome it all. But what I know now, and what I hope I've shared with you, is that the Bible does not say that forgiveness means staying in a relationship. It doesn't mean forcing yourself to say that you are okay when things in the relationship will never be okay again. It doesn't mean killing yourself to fulfill a command that God never gave.

If somebody comes up to me and asks, "Does Jesus really command us to forgive?" I have to say, "Yes, we read that in the New Testament, but what that really means is something far different from what we might have been taught it means." In the end, forgiveness happens when we can fully experience God's mercy for us.

I think, in the end, the forgiveness boot camp wasn't theologically necessary or the best frontline response to my desire for divorce. But I'll never forget or regret the time I spent sitting on the sofa in Penelope and Lucas's living room with muffins, tea, and, most important, company. I think all that was really required was stepping into the life that God wanted and was holding for me.

Step into that life. Do what it takes to get to that life. Maybe that life is different for you than it is for me. But know that life should be yours for the taking.

Forgiveness may follow, but I don't think it precedes.

So turn your face toward light, toward life, and take the brave first step, holding on to those who will walk this road with you.

You are beloved. Life should be yours.

acknowledgments

I would not have the opportunity to share this book with readers without the trust of Katelyn Beaty at Brazos Press and her entire team. Thank you for taking a chance on a relatively new writer without a big Instagram following. Thank you for knowing how important it was to share what I have learned through my experiences. Thank you for trusting me to tell my story—even though there is a risk to telling stories like mine.

Without my friend and pastor David Cramer, I most certainly would not have written this book. I am also not sure if, without David, I would be alive today, or at least really living. David, you stood with me in some of the hardest moments of my life. You told me that you believed me. You told me there was life. And you knew me well enough to know that one of the best ways for me to move toward that life was to write a book about everything.

My friends Penelope and Lucas (names changed) let me spend hours in their home when, without them, I'd have been incredibly lonely. You meant home and family to me, and you've probably seen me cry more than anyone else in the world. You got me thinking about forgiveness—especially after having me read a really problematic book about it. The process that unfolded in your living room changed many things for me.

I have been blessed with many conversation partners whose willingness to share and to dialogue with me contributed to this book. I won't name them all here, but if you've been part of my journey of writing this book, I thank you from the bottom of my heart. Especially to other survivors, thank you for trusting me with your brave stories. I will carry them with me always.

I expect that one day my daughters, Debbie, Gabby, and Rissa, will come across this book. Ladies, if you're reading this book, please know how deeply you are loved and how much your father and I love each other. Thank you for giving me hugs, cuddles, and kind words on the hard days. Being your mommy has been the greatest gift I've received, and I would never take back the roads that gave me you.

To my husband, Michael: you're the best thing I've ever found on the internet. Thank you for supporting me in our life together, through parenting our children, making delicious meals, surprising me with joy, making me laugh, and holding me. This book is not about your story, but I hope you know that I held your experiences in my heart as I typed each page. You are never alone. I'm grateful to God that our stories, though full of so much brokenness in the past, have intertwined and that together we have a new beginning and a hope.

All glory to God.

selected resources

Allison, Emily Joy. *#ChurchToo: How Purity Culture Upholds Abuse and How to Find Healing*. Minneapolis: Broadleaf Books, 2021.

Herman, Judith L. *Truth and Repair: How Trauma Survivors Envision Justice*. New York: Basic Books, 2023.

Larry, Susannah. *Leaving Silence: Sexualized Violence, the Bible, and Standing with Survivors*. Harrisonburg, VA: Herald, 2021.

Lerner, Harriet. *Why Won't You Apologize? Healing Big Betrayals and Everyday Hurts*. New York: Touchstone, 2017.

Maier, Bryan. *Forgiveness and Justice: A Christian Approach*. Grand Rapids: Kregel, 2017.

Mayo, Maria. *The Limits of Forgiveness: Case Studies in the Distortion of a Biblical Ideal*. Eugene, OR: Wipf & Stock, 2021.

Ramsay, K.J. *The Lord Is My Courage: Stepping Through the Shadows of Fear Toward the Voice of Love*. Grand Rapids: Zondervan, 2022.

Richardson, Jan. *The Cure for Sorrow: A Book of Blessings in Times of Grief*. Orlando: Wanton Gospeller, 2020.

Shoop, Marcia W. Mount. *Let the Bones Dance: Embodiment and the Body of Christ*. Louisville: Westminster John Knox, 2010.

Smith, Maggie. *Keep Moving: Notes on Loss, Creativity, and Change*. New York: One Signal, 2020.

Terkeurst, Lysa. *Good Boundaries and Goodbyes: Loving Others without Losing the Best of Who You Are.* Nashville: Thomas Nelson, 2022.

Thomas, Katherine Woodard. *Conscious Uncoupling: 5 Steps to Living Happily Even After.* New York: Harmony Books, 2015.

van der Kolk, Bessel. *The Body Keeps the Score: Brain, Mind, and Body in the Healing of Trauma.* New York: Penguin, 2015.

Williams, Delores S. *Sisters in the Wilderness: The Challenge of Womanist God-Talk.* Maryknoll, NY: Orbis Books, 1993.

notes

Chapter 1 Biblical Forgiveness(es)

1. Walter Brueggemann, "Forgiveness," in *Reverberations of Faith: A Theological Handbook of Old Testament Themes* (Louisville: Westminster John Knox, 2002), 87.

2. Brueggemann, "Forgiveness," 86.

3. In Luke 6:37, a line using a different word, *apoluo*, appears that links the related processes of offering and receiving forgiveness: "Do not judge, and you will not be judged; do not condemn, and you will not be condemned. Forgive, and you will be forgiven." Who is doing the forgiving here remains unspecified. God's forgiveness is not clearly withheld over a lack of human forgiveness.

4. For a more extended discussion of forgiveness in the Lord's Prayer, see Maria Mayo, "Community Cohesion or a Hegemony of Harmony?," in *The Limits of Forgiveness: Case Studies in the Distortion of a Biblical Ideal* (Eugene, OR: Wipf & Stock, 2021), 97–158.

5. Mayo, *Limits of Forgiveness*, 115.

6. This is a view I elaborate in my first book, where I discuss at length Jesus's situation of suffering trauma during his trial and subsequent death. See Susannah Larry, "Jesus and Sexualized Violence," in *Leaving Silence: Sexualized Violence, the Bible, and Standing with Survivors* (Harrisonburg, VA: Herald, 2021), 183–212.

Chapter 2 Anger

1. Bessel van der Kolk, *The Body Keeps the Score: Brain, Mind, and Body in the Healing of Trauma* (New York: Penguin, 2015), 29.

Chapter 3 Lament

1. McKenna Princing, "What You Need to Know about Toxic Positivity," *Right as Rain*, September 8, 2021, https://rightasrain.uwmedicine.org/mind/well-being/toxic-positivity.

2. Casey T. Sigmon, "'Blessed Is the One Whose Bowels Can Move': An Essay in Praise of Lament in Contemporary Worship," *Religions* 13, no. 12 (2022): 2.

3. Walter Brueggemann, "The Costly Loss of Lament," *Journal for the Study of the Old Testament* 36 (January 1986): 59–60.

4. Sigmon, "'Blessed Is the One,'" 3.

5. Brueggemann, "Costly Loss of Lament," 64.

Chapter 5 Reconciliation

1. The fact that details about my situation had been shared without my consent was itself a serious breach of confidence.

2. R. P. Martin, "Center of Paul's Theology," in *Dictionary of Paul and His Letters*, ed. Gerald F. Hawthorne and Ralph P. Martin (Downers Grove, IL: InterVarsity, 1993), 94.

3. H. Merkel, "καταλασσω," in *Exegetical Dictionary of the New Testament*, ed. Horst Balz and Gerhard Schneider, 2 vols. (Grand Rapids: Eerdmans, 1981), 2:263.

Chapter 6 Release and Rebirth

1. Delores S. Williams, *Sisters in the Wilderness: The Challenge of Womanist God-Talk* (Maryknoll, NY: Orbis Books, 1993), 127.

2. Enright's model of forgiveness uses release as a central element. See, for example, Robert D. Enright, Suzanne Freedman, and Julio Rique, "The Psychology of Interpersonal Forgiveness," in *Exploring Forgiveness* (Madison: University of Wisconsin Press, 1998). For a credible Christian understanding of forgiveness that incorporates release, see Bryan Maier, *Forgiveness and Justice: A Christian Approach* (Grand Rapids: Kregel, 2017).

Susannah Griffith is an independent scholar whose work focuses on the intersection of biblical studies and trauma. She is also a minister advocating and caring for the marginalized outside the walls of the church. Susannah's first book, *Leaving Silence*, was a *Christianity Today* Book Award finalist for Christian discipleship. She currently resides in Northern Indiana with her husband and three young daughters.